May 2016

Linda,
    Thank you for
your friendship over
the years!
        Love,
        Carole Sloan

And I Remember

Carolina S. Barr

Cover design art by: Brian K. Barr
Illustrations by: Gerardo Stecca
Editor: Tiff Stauffer
Copy Editor: Jennifer Lunde
Author Photo: Tiff Stauffer

ISBN-13: 978-1530285594

ISBN-10: 1530285593

CONTENTS

Part 2: Venezuela

FROM THE AUTHOR

As long as I can remember, my dad has told our family stories from his childhood. Most of them were funny, yet sometimes a sad one would sneak in. No matter how many times he told them, my siblings and I always loved them. A few years ago, Dad asked me if I would help him document his stories. I thought it was important that I help him, not only because I loved his narrative, but because I wanted to hand them down to my children and their children. Life teaches us so many lessons, whether they be through laughter or through tears. Each one of us has a story, and I wanted my dad's legacy to be remembered.

These anecdotes are true. The dates might not be exact because no child's memory is perfect. They portray the emotions, feelings, and sights of a world that most of us will never experience. Ranging from the war-stricken cities of Europe and the death that filled them, to the exotic jungles of a still-wild Venezuela, you will find yourself immersed. These stories will stir your emotions, just like they have always stirred mine. One moment, you will find yourself laughing at his teenage escapades while just a few chapters before, you were crying at the horrifying events WWII caused his young soul to experience.

Thank you, Dad, for sharing your life. You are my hero and I love you forever.

Carolina Barr

FOREWORD

Dade County
Miami, Florida
August 1992

We open the door of the small quarter-bath under our staircase. The six of us pile out, our eyes in awe at what we are seeing. The roof and some of the walls in our home are gone. Water on the floor is a few inches deep and drops are seeping through what remains of the second story floor. Everything inside our home is soaking wet and would soon contain the musky, dank odor of moisture that hangs heavy in the air. New "windows" are carved out in the remaining outer walls. I guess my wife always wanted more windows anyway. The home security alarm is still shrieking thanks to a powerful back-up battery. There is no phone service, neither land nor cellular. There is no running water, let alone electricity. We would soon discover that our clothing is lost or damaged, useless, and so are our shoes. We won't be able to flush the toilets because the water table and sewers are filled to the max. We have yet to realize our food is quickly spoiling and there is not enough clean drinking water available. We step outside and to our dismay, every house is damaged. Our neighborhood is completely destroyed.

All this was courtesy of Hurricane Andrew's visit during the early morning of August 24, 1992.

A few days later, help arrives. The National Guard and non-profit organizations begin the arduous task of distributing water and essential supplies. Our pharmacy was generous, not charging us for medication for the first few weeks after the storm. A large building materials store decided to help the community by only charging slightly above their cost for the much needed building supplies.

Neighbors helped with the absence of traffic lights. We helped with what we could. The less one had, the more one helped others. Of course, not everyone had the same good heart. There were looters, people cutting in the long gasoline lines and some surrounding counties with just minor damage gave us the cold shoulder. Last but not least, there were the endless amounts of fire ants and mosquitoes.

Once the sewers emptied some, flushing the toilet was a bit easier. We would use a bucket to get water from the endless amount of ponds and canals in South Florida. On one particular trip to the pond, I returned empty handed. I had no choice but to leave the bucket because I had accidentally thumped an alligator on its head.

All this was happening around me and I remembered…

The help we got after the total destruction and the hardships we experienced stimulated my memories; unbelievable memories of my childhood. There were some holes in these recollections but fortunately, my mother was still alive and I took the opportunity to ask her for the missing details. All the following stories about WWII are based on actual facts. These stories took place in Northern Italy, close to the Yugoslavian border: Trieste, Udine, Camporosso and Cividale during 1940-1948.

The alligators, mosquitoes, fire ants and the plethora of loose monkeys from the Miami Zoo and Monkey Jungle brought me back to my childhood in Venezuela, a place that was my home for 35 years.

The stories of my life in Venezuela are also based on real facts, and this is the reason I don't mention names. You will understand why once you read them. Some of them I can prove with the support of home movies, pictures and eye witnesses (unless, of course, they plead the fifth). These stories are from all over Venezuela. They range from the rainforest, high mountains, lakes, and rivers to the deserts, the Andes, Los Llanos (the plains) but mostly the Venezuelan coastline. During this time frame of 1948-1958 (with a few stories from the 60s), there were virtually no fishing regulations and only a few hunting laws. It was a time when environmental conservation did not exist. Pollution was unknown. Mosquitoes, flies, roaches, parasites, and the like were no strangers to this amazing tropical country. It was a time long gone, when a kid could truly be a kid.

But I am getting ahead of myself.

As this book opens up, I invite you to come and live my life with me, the best life I could have asked for. Just remember to bring your good sense of humor and a well-stocked first aid kit.

Yours Truly,
Gerardo Stecca

Part 1: Italy

FULVIO

Trieste, Northern Italy – WWII

I was born wet. Technically we are all born wet, I simply refused to dry. From the moment I entered this world, I was enthusiastically spraying everything and everyone who was brave enough to get close to my natural spigot. I wet myself, my bed, my diapers, my parents, my grandparents, and all things with which I came in contact. As I grew older, my perpetual state of moisture continued at home, the war shelter, school, movie theaters—even on bikes and in cars. I managed to spread moisture while standing, sitting, walking, running, rolling, jumping, eating, drinking, and sleeping. I could spray a straight line, sprinkler style, curved, or the ever-popular *raining shower*. My talent lasted until the ripe old age of seven, and the first five of those seven years were marked by WWII—providing my loved ones with added challenges during an already trying time.

Looking back now, I could place the blame for my wetting skills on the lack of bathrooms during the war. My father used our bathroom to house rather aggressive geese—I suspect that might also have played a part in my issue. Then again, maybe I had a small, hyperactive bladder. Perhaps I enjoyed the warmth, or maybe I enjoyed the desperate faces of those who had just fixed me up with a "dry" diaper. I even suspect that I'd begun to crave the attention and fame I was getting; I was becoming quite infamous.

Before my tale continues, I would like to clarify that diapers did not exist then as we know them today. At that time, diapers consisted of a white fabric that lacked the ability to absorb anything more than an ounce, and they leaked almost instantly. To make things even more interesting, washers and dryers were not available. All clothing, including my plethora of diapers, had to be hand-washed—a process involving cold water and homemade soap. The fortunate had a yard in which they could hang their laundry out to dry. Otherwise, one was forced to hang their laundry from their window and hope that no one would take it. Mom alternated between the two methods depending on where we were living.

I wonder now how my mom managed to always have a dry, clean diaper for me. I would often hear her say, "Please, do not pee right away. Stay nice and dry for a few minutes. You should be able to since you just peed."

My response was a casual, "You should not have said 'pee,'" because that always made me pee again.

My parents attempted to stop my leakage with several tactics: some scientific, some folklore, but mostly acts of desperation.

One day, my grandma came home with a big smile on her face. While in the ration card food line, she overheard a mother who had tamed her own wetting machine. That is when my grandma discovered a possible solution: Its name was Fulvio.

Fulvio would be the weapon used against me in the battle for dryness. He was a big, black, ragdoll rat, and his mission was simple: Before the offending child was tucked into bed, Fulvio was placed under the covers where he would lie in wait of his victim. The child was sternly assured that if he were to wet his bed, Fulvio would come and bite him. The dryness impaired child would then go to sleep; but at the first sign of moisture, a waiting family member would pull on a string attached to Fulvio and cause him to "scamper" across the bed. This would frighten the child right out of his bed-wetting tendencies. Or so my family thought.

My family's version of Fulvio was made by my grandma's talented hands. She improved the scary design by adding red buttons for eyes. Once her masterpiece was done and my bed was made, Fulvio was ready to pounce.

The night was like many other nights during WWII. Our town was under a mandatory curfew and blackout. This meant that moonlight was the only source of light. As I climbed into bed, my mother warned me one last time. "You are older now," she sighed. "You are almost a four-year-old. Please, do not wet your diapers and just let me know when you have to go. It's a very cold night, and I heard Fulvio might be in this neighborhood looking for a warm place to sleep. Please, DO NOT PEE THE BED!"

The moment she said 'pee,' I was not able to contain Niagara Falls; the waterworks began. My mom promptly removed my covers, and I watched through the moonlight as Fulvio made not one, but two mad dashes across my bed. Before I had time to react, the raid siren sounded, filling the air with intensity. As usual, the siren was too late and the air raid began simultaneously. Bombs dropped and exploded. Grandma picked up a few necessary things as my mom grabbed me. As we dashed to our basement shelter, I began to scream; the more my mother tried to calm me, the louder I became. It didn't take long for her to decipher my babbling and understand what I was shouting.

"MOM! Pull Fulvio by the string and don't leave him here alone! He could get hurt! I want to take him with me!"

The plan backfired—as plans often do when they involve tricking children. Attempting to scare me out of a childhood phase, my mom and grandma had inadvertently given me a new best friend. The war took much from us, and our possessions were few, but Fulvio remained with me for the duration of the war. He stayed despite the fact that I continued wetting everything with no mercy—including him.

SMOKING CHICKENS

Outskirts of Udine, Italy

I was a cute child. In fact, I was so cute that I won a contest in our town for being the cutest. My cuteness has grown into handsomeness over the years, but the fact that I have a newspaper article somewhere proving it still stands.

During this "age of cuteness", I recall living in a small two-story farm house. A green shuttered balcony protruded from the top floor. I remember it well. From it we witnessed the passing of many war planes and the exciting daredevil dog fights between the Allies and the opposing forces. Day or night, we would all huddle up in the balcony watching the war scene unfold in front of our eyes. During the darkness of night, we were able to gauge the closeness of the battle according to bright flashes and loud noises on the horizon. The excitement of watching such daring air acrobatics overpowered much of the fear I felt.

Directly across the road from us was a farm with a large home. Part of the home functioned as a small store where local villagers could buy homemade bread and fresh eggs. The yard around it was filled with chickens, clucking and scratching at the dirt below their feet. It was their turf and they knew it.

One day, my paternal grandfather came for a visit. I remember him as a chubby man with a thin mustache. He was loads of fun, but always distracted and forgetful, not that that mattered to my youthful heart. Unfortunately, his distractibility eventually led to his death when he accidentally drank contaminated brandy while in a bomb shelter.

I adored him and we had a special bond marked by a unique tradition of hanging a pair of cherries from our ears. This day, like many others, I found great joy in pretending they were expensive pendants. Despite the fact I knew they were simple cherries picked from our tree, they were worth so much more when he gave them to me.

Shortly and suddenly after his arrival, a group of airplanes came flying over our home. This was normal activity to us but this particular chase had come closer than any other and all at once I was filled with excitement. I stopped what I was doing to gaze up at the sky above. One of the planes was shot down as he zoomed above our heads. Smoke began to consume the air as our ears filled with the high-pitched squeals of the plane going down.

Within a split second and to the horror of everyone there, we realized the plane was headed directly towards us. The adults began to shout and signal at others, their arms flailing in the air in a desperate attempt to warn everyone. I knew we didn't have much time so I ran as fast as my little legs could carry me. We took cover in the house and before we could find safer shelter, we were overwhelmed by a loud explosion. Everything around us shook. My ears immediately began to pulse and all I could hear was muffled sounds and an intense ringing from within. It was so disorienting, it took a while to get my bearings back and see the fire billowing from the farm house across the road. We were safe!

Stepping out of the safety of our home, we inched our way closer to the wreck and began assessing the situation. Through the smoke, I could see a parachute tangled in what remained of the plane's tail side. The pilot had tried to eject, but we believed that because he had been dog-fighting at a low elevation, he did not make it. The heat of the fuel-fed fire destroyed all evidence identifying the plane. We didn't know if he had been friend or foe.

What I do know is the carefree days were over for those proud chickens. In the panic and destruction, they had been scattered. I could see a great deal of them running around; some with feathers on their bodies and others without. Every single one was smoking and on fire. I can guarantee the casualties were many and few lived to run another day.

I only I wish I could remember what we had for dinner that evening.

A SAD, SAD NIGHT

Udine, Italy

A four-year-old's brain is like a sponge, absorbing all of its surroundings and taking in any detail that could be useful in the future. Some statements, such as mom saying "you can play later", would be stored into memory and used frequently to remind said mother that playtime had been promised. Kids this age also have a small section in their brain called "selective memory." This is where they store commands such as "clean your room" and "don't hit your sister", commands they know but don't necessarily demonstrate that they comprehend.

There are also certain memories that don't belong in either of these categories. These recollections are permanently written on the brain with an ink that no doctor, medicine or natural disaster could erase. These memories aren't pleasant. As a matter of fact, they are on the opposite side of the scale. They are memories a person often prays would leave them but instead, plague the brain like an incurable disease.

A certain difficult night in my childhood falls into this last category. The memory of this night came rushing back to me fourteen years after it occurred when I was living in Venezuela. The government was conducting a civil defense drill that included search lights and tracer bullets, and in an instant, I remembered the terrible night.

During my youngest years, my family lived in Udine (pronounced *OO d ee neh*). This relatively large city, located in northeastern Italy between the Adriatic Sea and the majestic Alps, was beautiful before it was ravaged by war. Our city had already seen its share of destruction, ranging from battles in its early days of conquests to natural disasters such as the 1511 earthquake. But no prior destruction was as devastating as a world war. Time eventually healed the landscape, but the historical buildings were never the same.

That fateful night in Udine was pitch-black dark. The only lights visible through our window were that of the tracer bullets coming from snipers. They crossed the night sky and went over rooftops and beyond. I could hear sounds and screams coming in through the cracks under the door and around the windows. I was commanded to stay away from windows; the risk of those bullets going astray always kept us all away. I could hear all sorts of voices calling "*Mamma! Aiuto* (Help me, mom)!" They were screams of desperation. They were shouts of pain.

I could not fathom what the cries really meant. All I knew was war. My surroundings both scared and excited me. My life thus far was a normal state of fear and excitement over planes dog-fighting, endless search lights, explosions and tracer bullets galore. This particular night was not an exception to that routine.

As the night progressed, sleep got the better of me and I drifted into it willingly. I awoke from a restless slumber to find my parents, along with some friends, looking outside. Their whispers filled the room. I rubbed the sleep out of my eyes and observed that the faces of the adults were wrought with horror and grief. Their distraction was enough to allow me to creep up beside them unnoticed. By the time their warnings reached my ears, it was too late.

I saw bodies. They hung from the windows of the building across the street. Silent and not moving, the bodies and the walls around them were covered in a dark, oozing liquid. I was pulled away but the damage had been done. Years later, my parents would explain what I had seen.

There had been an attack on a German garrison, provoking a brutal retaliation. Innocent men and women, Italians, were hung by their lower jaws by meat hooks. The hooks penetrated the bottom of their jaws and protruded out of their mouths. The friends and family of those poor murdered souls were the snipers I heard that night. Those bullets came from loved ones who only sought to end the suffering.

I wish I could forget.

THE LITTLE MOUSE
AND THE GEESE

Udine, Italy

Life in Udine during WWII brought many challenges, but my early childhood included many positive memories that I enjoy pondering to this day. My father worked as a railroad engineer, entitling us to live in a second floor apartment owned by the railroad company. It was a small dwelling and when I say small, I mean small. It included a tiny kitchen, an all-inclusive family/living/dining room, one bedroom and an itty-bitty bathroom. The dining area contained a window under which our table sat. I would often sit on this table and look out upon the gardens and the potpourri of buildings surrounding us. It was a place where a young boy could find his imagination and dream of what the outside world held. From this height, I was the king of my world, looking out over my domain.

That same window was where I lost my first tooth.

The tooth had been quite burdensome and loose for some time. It was barely hanging on, which made me cry periodically in fear. The looser it became, the more frightened my wails were. In my little mind, this process could only end in serious pain.

One afternoon, Dad came home after an extremely long day at the train yard. He was exhausted and covered in soot. Needless to say, he was desperately in need of rest from the demands of the day. Unfortunately, he did not choose a very peaceful moment to come home. The second he walked through the door, he was drawn into the drama I was causing over this tooth. It was the last thing he needed, but he was a good dad. He attempted to calm me down but the sight of him, unshaven and covered in coal, frightened me even more. His scary appearance led me to reach the highest level of screeching possible. If my mom had owned any crystal wine glasses, I would surely have shattered them. No opera singer could have outdone my high-pitched shrieks that day.

Mom also tried calming my flailing body, but she wasn't able do any better than my poor dad. Try as they might, it seemed like a hopeless situation. I sat on our table in a panicked state as my parents tried to figure out how to help.

Whether it was a light bulb going off or divine intervention, my dad soon found the solution to my distress. He gave me one his ever-loving and gentle whacks on my behind, causing the tooth to fly right through that window. My first tooth, lost forever in the abyss. The tooth was out without any pain but it was a different story for my parents. In their desperation, they failed to foresee that I would begin a new form of frantic wails. My tooth had been lost and the realization of not having a visit from the little tooth mouse (Italy's version of the tooth fairy) was too much for my little heart to bear. I don't know how my parents survived that night. Eventually, my tantrum wore me out and I fell into a deep sleep. The next day, I awoke to a wonderful miracle. The little tooth mouse had found his way to me even without the tooth itself and all was well in the world.

That apartment held more memories than the infamous tooth, as you will soon learn. Now think back to the story I told about my ability to pee on command. I mentioned possible reasons for my problem, one being the lack of bathrooms not contain geese.

One good day, as good as days could be during a world war, Dad came home with a strange group. I recognized the four men with him, but the two unknown members of the group caught my attention. They were quite strange, different than the others. Upon further examination, I realized they were geese.

They were huge, aggressive, mean-looking and in need of some serious tranquilizers. Their size was remarkable; they were taller than I was. My dad was quick to point out that one day these beasts would be our dinner. The war deprived us and everyone else of much needed nourishment. When the opportunity to eat something other than pigeon and cat came along, my dad jumped at the chance. It was difficult being hungry, but not as heart-wrenching as seeing your children hungry. These geese were an answered prayer!

In order for them to provide us with a few days of much needed nutrition, our new roommates would have to be fattened up. The fattening was completed by force feeding the geese through a funnel. The task would have to be performed often and would require a bit of time. It was diligent work that would one day pay off. Our commitment was strengthened with the thought of how delicious they would taste.

This whole geese-as-food thing was a nice idea, but there were questions that ran through my frightened mind. Where would we house our food and how long before we could eat them? Would I have to share my bed? My dad was quick to answer. The length of time could not be measured. It would be as long as it would take until they were fattened up. So, where would they stay? In our bathroom, of course! I had no say on the matter. Our bathroom would become a new battle field, not full of German SS soldiers, but oversized and angry geese.

This leads me to one of my hypotheses about my wetting problems. How could someone expect a scared little boy to go wee-wee in a bathroom containing two bullying geese? I think I can rest my case. There can be no other explanation.

And just in case you are wondering, they tasted delicious!

THE TRAIN

Udine, Italy

My dad was an engineer on a coal-steam locomotive. His primary duty was to drive a long cargo train between Udine and Yugoslavia and sometimes beyond. I remember his face and hands were always coated with a thick charcoal residue. It's an image that to this day brings to mind hard work. My dad's hours were long, and he often worked while sick and without food. The rations were meager, which quite often lead to illness. At one point in time, he even worked while suffering from Scarlett Fever. Sick leave did not exist back then and there were no unions to protect the worker. You either worked or you starved.

Dad was a clever man and was almost always able to find food for himself during his long trips. He often ate onions, dandelions and small birds when no other food could be found. He always made sure there was food on our table at home. This food was not a meal to be admired, but it did the trick and kept us as healthy as we could be during a time when Europe was deprived. Our diet consisted of, and was limited to: small birds, cats too slow to get away from us, dandelions, and small potatoes we gleaned after fields were harvested. Staples such as bread were rationed and it was nearly impossible to obtain such things as eggs and meat. The prices were exorbitant and most common folk like us could not afford such luxuries. We never knew how she did it, but Mom always managed to get butter for us little ones and despite the fact that it was always rancid, we enjoyed our treat.

One particular evening after work, Dad came home with a very sad face. He looked beaten emotionally, bad enough that I took notice. I overheard his conversation with my mom and quickly learned the reason behind his melancholy. He had been ordered to drive a train car full of people to work camps. My parents knew well what happened in those "work camps." It was the last thing he wanted to do, but those dreaded tasks could not be avoided. Refusing would cost you your life, or, even worse, the lives of those you loved.

The following day, Dad reluctantly left for work. Gloom hung over our home. His long journey would not bring him back for a few days. As the day wore on, we settled into our daily routines, knowing that time would crawl by as we waited for his return. Yet much to our surprise, Dad walked into our house that very evening. It was always good to see him safely home, but I could see the concerned look on Mom's face.

My parents greeted each other and soon, began their whispering. I caught a few words with my sharp ears: "derailed...dangerous...people."

War has many ways of causing a child to grow up faster than they should. Because of this, I understood the meaning of this conversation. My dad had done something good and I was glad he was home and my family was complete once again.

Little did I know, my dad had managed to piss off the German SS. Really piss them off. As my mother explained to me a few years later, his cargo had been a great deal of people, mostly Jews, and his destination had been a concentration camp. What offended the SS so greatly was that my dad intentionally derailed the train. His actions caused a great deal of the "cargo" to escape and that didn't sit well with the SS at all.

We all know good friends are hard to come by, and on that day Dad truly understood what that meant. One of my father's friends took it upon himself to disclose the derailment to the German SS. Not only did he tell them about that particular night, he told them my dad had done this twice.

I didn't see my dad for a few nights after that fateful evening. He disappeared not only to protect himself, but us as well. He returned home one evening, unshaven and dirty. In his hands, there was a rifle. He was accompanied by a group of people I had never met before, the Partigiani – the Italian resistance. My dad had been in hiding and the resistance had helped him. The Partigiani opposed the occupying German forces and the Italian Socialist Republic regime during the war. The resistance was formed by pro-Ally Italians during the German military invasion of Northern Italy. They were the good guys. Their visit was short and my dad soon left again because the German SS were still looking for him.

A day or so after the brief visit with Dad, another air raid alarm sounded. Mom and I were out in town and began frantically running for shelter. I don't recall whether my brother had been born yet, but I do clearly remember holding her hand as we ran for cover. Udine was under heavy bombardment coming from all directions of the sky above. In the midst of the chaos, we were abruptly stopped by some German men wearing a uniform displaying the SS emblem. I can only imagine the desperate thoughts going through my mom's head. They arrested my mom upon identifying her and swiftly and took her away, leaving me stranded in the middle of the street, scared and alone. Bombs were exploding. Fires had already burned down many buildings all around me. I was alone. I was afraid and barely four years old.

Out of nowhere, two hands lifted me up. I suddenly found myself in the arms of an SS soldier. After witnessing what the SS emblem meant and was capable of doing, you can image the fear in my little heart. I couldn't run from his strong grip. Even if I did, where would I go in a city falling apart with destruction? There was nothing I could do but surrender.

After he picked me up, the soldier placed his weighty helmet upon my head. He carried me for a while, knocking on every door that remained standing. When he tired, he handed me off to others in his unit and they proceeded to do the same. They knocked for what must have been hours until finally, they knocked upon a house belonging to my great-grandfather. There, they gently handed me over and left. These soldiers, who were often commanded to do horrible things, saved me. In that instant, I saw that not all had the same evil heart that their leaders had. They were someone's son, brother, father, friend. There was still hope.

GREAT GRANDPA'S HOUSE

Udine, Italy

I stayed with my great-grandparents for a while, but because time passes differently for a child, I cannot properly recall the length of time I was there. My best guess is that I remained with them between one and five weeks until my parents came for me. Mom was released from jail and my dad eventually found it was safe to come out of hiding.

It only took me a short while before I became comfortable in my temporary abode. Great-grandpa's house was a simple two-story dwelling made of stones and lumber. The downstairs room was multi-purpose serving as a kitchen, family room, dining area, and anything else that did not involve sleeping. There was a large table surrounded by several chairs with wiggly straw-filled pillows. The kitchen range and oven consisted of a large caldron hung over a fire fueled by wood and coal. In the cauldron and the few black pans in the kitchen, my grandma cooked staple meals such as soups, polenta, raw milk, pasta and potatoes.

I loved my great-grandmother's cooking. She always managed to make something delicious out of nothing. Her polenta was something to be admired, but it was quite a challenge making it. The preparation of polenta requires constant care and stirring. This was no easy feat, since the cauldron it was cooked in was directly over a blazing fire. My great-grandma would bend over it as she stirred the thick mixture until it reached a perfect consistency. This led to a lot of sweating. The beads of perspiration would run down her nose, intermixing with the drops coming out of her nostrils and into the polenta they would go. I didn't mind. I would never turn away something that tasted so good when topped with hot, sweet milk.

The stairs in the simple house served two purposes; a passageway to the bedrooms and an easy way to scare the hell out of me. My fear was a result of a full-body life-size statue located in the landing just as you turned right. This statue was much bigger than I and of a dark brown color. It was old and worn out and I could barely make out what it was supposed to be. It looked like some sort of a saint statue you might find in an old church. It was even scarier at night when I would climb the stairs, my path lit by candlelight. The spooky shadows it cast chilled my soul.

While living in my great-grandparents' house, I was very grateful to be male. I say this because the bathroom was an outhouse. I was glad that I could use a small bed pan under my bed instead of having to tread out in the cold like my poor great-grandma did. I got the feeling my great-grandpa shared the same sentiments as I on the matter.

The yard contained a small farm. My great-grandpa cultivated it and we enjoyed figs, grapes, cherries, potatoes, cabbage and other delicious fruits and vegetables. It was enjoyable to always have something fresh on the table. I would often find big glass jars filled with cherries or grappa (a grape-based alcoholic beverage) that my great-grandpa would leave out to ferment as he worked the land. I even showed him how to place cherries behind his ears just like my grandpa (his son) had shown me.

I found a few special hideouts for myself on the farm. The grape vines were great for times I wanted to hide from the world. My second hideout was the fig tree. Even though I was too small to climb it, I loved going to it because there was always a dark purple sweet treat waiting for me to pick.

Our small farm was fenced in. On the other side of that fence was an old two-story house. I don't recall what it was, perhaps a school or an orphanage; but I do remember there were many children living there. During one of the bombings, I remember hearing a very loud explosion behind the house. The next day, I went out exploring as usual but noticed there were pieces of what looked like raw beef scattered everywhere, even on my great-grandfather's glass jars. For some reason, I can only remember this as if I were watching a black and white movie. No color, just black and white. I noticed the house with the children was destroyed and there was no one around. I'm so grateful that at that time, I didn't understand what I was really looking at. Many memories are worth cherishing. This one, I wish I could forget.

All of the memories of how I came to be at my great-grandpa's house and my time there came flooding back to me in 2010, as my daughter and her two sons joined my wife and I on a visit to a local train yard. An old charcoal locomotive, now converted to diesel oil, was undergoing some repairs. Its heavy, black engine sat still. My grandchildren were excited as they climbed the steep, slippery ladder to explore the many gauges and blow the whistle. This is when I found myself holding back emotions I had stored deep inside so many years ago. Emotions that led me back to my great-grandpa's house, to my father and the train derailments, to the bombings, and into the SS soldier's strong arms.

A GOOD DOG

Outskirts of Udine, Italy

We spent quite a bit of our time in Italy moving from home to home, mostly due to the war. If our home was destroyed during a bombing, we alternated between temporary housing and living with family. I'm sure this was difficult on my parents, but for us kids each new home brought a new adventure.

During this time in my life I was a big brother. My younger brother had been born two years prior and although he was little and more of a nuisance than anything, I loved him. I decided it would be fine if my parents kept him. I was sure that one day, he would come in handy.

Our house was a large two-story home with a small farm attached to it. I loved that place. I particularly enjoyed watching the swallows fluttering in and out of the spaces between the old tiles on the roof. In the early spring they were busy building their nests, and it wasn't long before the sounds of young chirping would fill the air.

Like most houses in the area, the large back yard contained our own outhouse. It was small, private and very stinky. The house itself was very bright inside. The large dark-wood trimmed windows were covered with white curtains detailed with small red flowers. The geraniums my mom kept on the windowsill complimented them well.

The house was made complete by the smells coming from the kitchen. My mom always had something cooking and no matter what it was, she managed to make it smell delicious. I was constantly at her heels, trying to get a taste of whatever masterpiece she was cooking. The kitchen had a fair amount of onion and garlic wreaths that added to the hominess.

On one fateful day, my mother had to leave. I can't recall the reason why but it must have been important because my mom always made sure we were taken care of. She would not have left us kids alone unless it was absolutely necessary. As she said goodbye, she brought in our huge, mean-looking dog to keep us company. I wasn't too comfortable around him because, like most animals, he was much bigger than I was.

From the moment she left, I sat with my face pressed against the window, waiting for her return. I was getting pretty good at waiting, but it didn't make things any easier. When you are five, things always seem to take forever. This fact is particularly true when you have a large dog staring at you.

For quite a while, the scenery outside didn't change much. Time ticked by and I soon found myself looking at a German SS soldier and a pair of German Shepherd dogs moving in the direction of our front door. Out of instinct and possibly safety training from my parents, I ducked to make myself invisible. Our dog, as mean as he was, did the same as if knowing that danger was on the other side of the door. My brother was oblivious to it all as he lay sleeping peacefully.

It was then that the knocking began. I froze. Not even a hair on my head moved. Despite how quiet we were, the knocking grew louder and louder. The soldier did not seem to be getting the hint to go away. After a few minutes, I figured he wouldn't stop so I stood and began making my way towards the front door. I suddenly found my path blocked by our dog. He was quiet and stood his ground. He showed me his canines, telling me that he meant business. I didn't dare take his challenge so once again, I froze.

The knocking on the door continued to grow in intensity and soon turned into banging. My heart was pounding and starting to beat faster when I noticed that my baby brother began to show signs of waking up. Our dog continued to block my path to the door. I could see the shadows of the soldier trying to peek through the window panels that blocked his view. I was scared and wanted my mom.

It felt like an eternity had passed but just as suddenly as he had appeared, the soldier left. It was over and I knew that we were safe once again. I went back to waiting for my mom, but this time, I chose to stay away from the window.

As soon as my mother came home, I frantically told her about our experience during her absence. She had to sit down, almost fainting at the thought of what could have happened if I had opened that door. No one could tell for sure what the soldier planned on doing or what he wanted with us. Maybe he was just on patrol or maybe he had come to collect us. I will never know.

What I do know is that my mom called our dog a hero. From that day on, he didn't look so mean to me and I soon found I had a new best friend.

THE FORGOTTEN LITTLE SHEEP

Udine, Italy

It was a clear day. I remember looking up at the fluffy clouds scattered in the sky, making out shapes of little sheep. I was a typical five-year-old enjoying the task of identifying cloud shapes. I think every child enjoys days when he can use his imagination and create a whole world in the sky.

Not far from where I lay, adults sat listening to the news. The war had been dragging on for six years. It was all I had ever known. I was born during the war and I had somehow lived through it. It was my "normal."

The radio announcer was detailing the last effort by the Nazis to hold on to Berlin. The only ones left fighting were children. I could clearly envision the children - fighting with heavy guns and getting hurt. The picture the announcer was painting was vividly clear in my head. Death was an everyday event in the world I lived in. I considered myself a five-year-old war veteran, scars and all.

The grown-ups were usually quiet during the war report. They intently listened and absorbed every word the announcer spoke as if their lives depended on it. I noticed the intensity but I was young and didn't realize that yes, our lives did depend on it. We relied on updated information of where the latest attacks were. We could then judge our safety and if our family members in different cities were in danger.

The report ended and the intense silence was broken. The excitement and shouting coming from the adults snapped me from my sheep-cloud imaginings. I tuned my ears in to what they were boisterously proclaiming.

The war was over.

Just like that, we were free. No more bombings, no more running, no more hiding, no more fear. Tears of joy flowed and it was as if the world stopped spinning and let out a big sigh of relief.

The American soldiers remained in Europe through June 1947, allowing the ailing cities to heal and get back on their feet. Their presence was a comfort to us. To this day, the sight of a soldier brings me peace and joy. I will forever be grateful to the GIs.

It was over, yet…

I have not forgotten the little sheep in the sky.

I have not forgotten those children. They died fighting for a lost cause, but they fought.

I have not forgotten the Allies who, in their horror and sorrow, crushed the Nazis so that the nightmare could end.

I will never forget.

SCHOOL

Outskirts of Udine, Italy

The war was over. Winter, spring and summer passed. Fall brought a new experience for me and I couldn't wait to get to go to school for the first time. I was looking forward to learning anything and everything the teacher could throw at me. There were no words to describe my excitement. The sentiment was the same for my mom who was most likely looking forward to a break from my ever-present curiosity.

Our school uniform consisted mostly of a black sort of toga covering most of my body. Two broad white bands wrapped around the top part of the right sleeve, indicating my grade level.

I had not been able to attend school during the war. Instead, my schooling was done at home by my parents. War had a way of interrupting life, so I was taught whenever time allowed. I loved history. My favorite things to learn about were Egypt, pyramids, and the pharaohs of time gone by. Egyptian history has a way of capturing the imagination of little boys. My mind ran wild with visions of mummies, archeologists and powerful kings that ruled the ancient world. Mom did most of the teaching except for math; that was Dad's job. I loved how much there was to learn!

An evaluation test was used to determine whether or not I was ready to attend regular school. Its results revealed what grade, if any, I would be placed in. My parents accompanied me when the day of the test arrived. I was a little nervous but the excitement of starting school was greater. The test wasn't long and we soon found out the results: I would be starting in second grade. My parents' pride swelled upon hearing I would be skipping a grade! Was I a genius? Hardly. It turned out I wasn't the only one ahead of the game. A few more local children joined in the honors. That didn't stop my parents from being proud of me.

My backpack was nothing to be prized. It was small, but contained all the bare necessities any genius like myself would require: food, a pencil, a pen with a few spare tips and a brand new notebook. I must have packed and unpacked that bag dozens of times in the days leading to the first day of class.

My school was located at the end of the road. It was a short walking distance that led me across a field and around a few bombardments and I was there. Mom had the privilege of walking me to school on my first day. Upon our arrival, we quickly spotted the teacher. She was a tall, skinny woman dressed in a simple black dress. Her face was as stern as they came and I remember that her eyes were sad. It was a look many had in war-ravaged Europe. She imposed respect and discipline. I had mixed feeling about her and decided not to make up my mind on whether or not I liked her just yet. I would give her a few days to prove she was as good as my mom.

The classroom was simple. It had a few rectangular windows, taller than they were wide. We came in through the entrance just right of the teacher's desk, which was slightly elevated from the rest of the classroom by a wooden platform. I noted the fireplace on the same side as the door, giving me some relief that I would not be freezing during the cold, winter months.

"So far, so good," I thought.

I soon found my desk. It was old with an inkwell and a small groove to place my pen. Pencils were strictly meant for drawing and nothing else and therefore did not have a home on the desk. The room began to slowly fill with fellow classmates, each with their own personality. There were happy, shy, loud, quiet and some sorrowful kids. Not all seemed as excited to be there as I was.

Our school session began shortly after what seemed like hours of instructions from the teacher. She explained the school and classroom rules, the types of punishments for different bad behaviors (usually involving a good whack with a ruler) and other necessary instructions that would make our school experience run smoothly. I sat as still as possible and tried my hardest to listen, but all my mind wanted to do was to think about all the things I could be learning about.

I loved to write with my pen on my new notebook. With every writing assignment, we were asked to include a drawing. The pages of the little notebook alternated one with little squares for math problems and the next had lines for writing. We were not allowed to have any marks, other than what we wrote or drew on the paper. Everything had to be perfect with no ink spots or eraser marks. It was an important detail that needed to be followed in order to be accepted into the third grade. It's a habit that remains with me to this day. My, how times have changed!

We were graded on a scale from 0 to 10 on each subject. A "10" would always be what we were to aim for. Getting a "0" would mean total failure leading to a reprimand from your teacher and often a harsh response at home. While the choice punishment tool at school was a ruler, a nice belt would most likely be used by frustrated parents.

Needless to say, I was motivated by both sides to always do my best.

It wasn't long after the school year began that I chose how I felt about my teacher. She ended up being a very sweet, mild and soft spoken person. She would hardly ever resort to using the ruler as punishment and when she did, it was usually administered in a very gentle manner. Looking back now, her demeanor was most likely due to much suffering during the war. It made both rulers and belts much lighter than they were before.

As time went by, I was eventually allowed to walk to school by myself. This, of course, came with a few mishaps. On one exceptionally cold day, I headed to school wearing some very itchy underwear. The reason for the itching was that on my way, I was crossing the field without paying attention and fell into a bomb crater that had been covered in snow. It was deep enough to soak my underwear. My little wet body eventually made it all the way to school without any further incidents.

As I walked into my classroom, the warmth of the fireplace flowed over my entire body. Can you guess what happened next? An overwhelming feeling came over me and I couldn't hold it in any longer: I peed in front of the entire class. A river of tears followed as the thought of being teased filled my mind. My teacher was quick to come to my rescue. She took me aside and handed me a blanket. The little toga that went on top of our uniform was dry so with that over me and the blanket around me, I was able to attend class. All the while, my pants, underwear, socks and coat hung close to the fireplace and were ready just in time for me to walk home. Not one of my classmates made fun of me. Thank you, friends, and a special thank you to Bevilacqua, the only classmate I remember by name.

SPAM - THE OTHER, OTHER WHITE MEAT

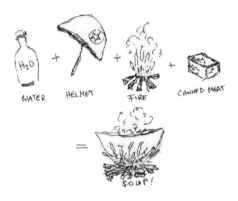

Udine, Italy

Picture a big, rustic wooden table in the middle of a crowded outdoor eating area. This table was a gathering place for my family along with other locals, where we would enjoy a meal together. Our fare of choice was polenta. I use the word "choice" loosely, as rations were low and our selection of post-war meals was limited. So, polenta it was.

Polenta is a traditional Italian dish, and at the time it was christened "the food of the poor". It is made of cornmeal boiled in salt water until thickened to a porridge-like consistency. It is a versatile dish and can be eaten with honey, butter, or tomato sauce, all of which we didn't have most of the time.

As we sat around the table preparing to enjoy our feast, one of the men pulled out a treasure he had received from an American soldier. This treasure sat in front of us: a huge cracker and two tins, one round and large and the other square. None of us knew what the contents of the tins were and we had not been trained in the proper use of them.

It was then that my dad was nominated as the one to assess this mysterious bounty.

The first item was obviously a cracker, he informed us. It was square and so hard that one could use it to drive a nail through concrete. Dad bravely gave it a bite but he nearly lost a tooth.

"*Non buono!*" he shouted. No good!

The square tin came next. After carefully observing it, Dad punched a small hole on the top using his knife. A clear liquid oozed from the tiny hole. Not satisfied with his findings, he proceeded to make a larger hole and was finally able to remove the entire top. A jelly-like mass of animal fat covered what looked like meat. It certainly did look like food, but it did not smell good.

The verdict was another resounding "*Non buono!*"

The large, round tin was easier to open. It had what looked like a little key on its top but I couldn't see the keyhole anywhere. I was puzzled but sat quietly and watched my dad's next move with much anticipation. He used his knife once again to uncover the tin's contents. We all stared at the white powder inside as Dad took a reluctant taste. He reported the sweetness of it and the fact that it stuck to the roof of his mouth, like some sort of powdered ice cream.

"*Non buono!*" he proclaimed, this time slamming his fist on the table.

We stared at the items. We weren't sure how anyone could eat it without losing a tooth, gagging on fat or gluing their intestines. It was puzzling.

Our predicament was witnessed by a few GIs, who feeling pity towards us, were kind enough to come to our rescue. One of the soldiers cleaned his helmed and filled it with hot water. Without speaking, he sliced the contents of the square tin and placed a few slices into the helmet. He soaked the brick-like cracker until it became soft. Giving me a quick wink, he grabbed a spoon and began to eat his creation.

Meanwhile, another soldier scooped a few teaspoons of the white powder into a cup of hot water, stirred it and said something sounding like "Moo milk". I peeked into his cup and realized that he had made milk right in front of my eyes! I looked up at my dad in anticipation of what his final judgement would be.

"*Buono!*" he declared with a resounding laugh.

It was a glorious day! We enjoyed our meal together and soon learned that our food repertoire had been expanded by what the GIs called Spam, powdered milk and hard-tack. We were grateful for the addition to our food choices but most of all, we were thankful to our friendly and often funny American friends.

IL DOTTORE

Udine, Italy

At eight years old, I was living the good life. We had a new house just outside of Udine across La Roia, a small river. Mom was very happy with our new abode and everything was going well. It was close to Udine, but far away enough for us to enjoy a semi-farm life. I loved the school I was attending and Dad was happy working at a restaurant he owned, despite the fact he didn't know anything about cooking. I found enjoyment in my little brother and although he had previously been just a nuisance, he had somehow developed into a good friend.

One beautiful day, I was approached by my mother. She was wearing a reassuring smile as she asked me to tag along on a trip to town. Going to town was always an adventure, so I eagerly agreed to join her. Although memories of Udine often elude me, the location of this particular experience on that fateful day will remain with me until eternity.

We walked up to a building, just like any other building on that street. Mom knocked on the door and we were ushered into a small room. There, we were greeted by a nice dark-haired woman in a white dress. She politely asked me to take a seat in a chair oddly placed in the middle of the room.

I was in a good mood, having had an adventure to the city, so I obliged and sat down where I was told. Almost immediately, the "nice and polite" woman began tying me to the chair. The smile quickly faded from my face and my instincts told me this was not a good situation. Red flags began to wave in my mind's eye. The panic set in once I looked upon my mom's face. She was quietly crying into her hands. No, this did not look good at all.

Meanwhile, Il Dottore – the doctor – snuck up behind me and began to tie my head to the chair with a belt he most likely had taken off his own trousers. I couldn't figure it out. What was this all about? And why was Il Dottore wearing a funny white mask over his mouth and nose?

As he walked around the chair, the masked doctor looked intently into my eyes and asked me to open my mouth. Even though every ounce of me wanted to open it so I could scream for help, I knew that doing so would only bring me more trouble. I resisted with a mumbled "no," followed by a bunch of exclamation points.

He looked at me once again and repeated his request: "Open your mouth!"

I did not move a muscle. If I had thought I could escape I would have, but there was no way of undoing the belts and straps that held me down.

Il Dottore did not give up so easily. I watched his mind work and a few seconds later, felt the sharpness of his slap across my face. Out of pure instinct, I finally opened my mouth to let out a scream of pain. That was my undoing. He saw his opportunity and quickly placed a piece of metal into my mouth so I could not close it again.

Nope, this did not look good!

Meanwhile, my poor mom kept sobbing as she watched helplessly from the corner of the room. In all of the chaos, I had failed to notice that the white-clad woman had left the room. She reentered carrying a tray with some ominous looking instruments, a mound of cotton balls, a kind of wound dressing and some small pewter bowls. I quickly spotted the only device I recognized – a syringe. At this point, panic kicked into full gear. I knew there was no turning back from something painful.

Il Dottore looked into my mouth as his hands quickly armed themselves with various instruments. The woman in white reached out for a bowl and gently placed it under my chin. That would be the last gentle movement from either of those two characters.

Straining my eyes to see out of their corners, I saw a large metal device start entering my ever-screaming mouth. Within a minute, but not fast enough in my opinion, two bloody ball-looking things were placed inside the bowl. I felt a warm, gooey liquid flood down my chin. My screams continued and I am sure they were heard miles away. They might have even been mistaken as bomb sirens by someone still recuperating from the war. Then, it was all over.

Many times, we hear statements claiming how kids bounce back from trauma faster than adults. Well, I know I did. Less than an hour after my adenoids were removed without any anesthesia (due to the shortages of WWII, it was not commonly used), I happily walked home holding my mom's hand and a huge ice cream cone. One hour later, I was joyfully kicking around the new soccer ball Mom had bought me, probably out of guilt, despite having been strictly ordered to rest by Il Dottore.

I did feel some burning during the operation, but it wasn't anything terribly painful. Who knows? Perhaps my pain was even scared off by my screaming.

I don't believe my mom blamed me for not going to the follow-up appointment. Or was it that she did not want to face Il Dottore after all the kicking and screaming I did? The reason didn't matter to me. I just wanted to be left alone with my ice cream and new soccer ball.

TRIUMPH

Udine & Trieste, Italy

In order to attend my uncle's wedding in Trieste, my dad and I had to undertake a long road trip. This would be yet another joyful excursion in my short life, particularly since we would make this journey on an old Triumph motorcycle. Dad loved his huge, powerful bike as much as he hated its tires. They were covered in patches and had seen better days. He hadn't upgraded them in a while, thinking they still had plenty of life left in them. Even though the war was over, it was still difficult to find decent tires and inner tubes. The only source for obtaining them was the American and British soldiers who frequented Dad's restaurant, *Ristorante Il Cavallino Rosso.*

When the big day came, we left our home in Udine at dawn. We began our trip without giving our tires a second thought. The trip took a few hours and despite the fact that Dad didn't attach the side car to save on gas, my face beamed with joy as I sat behind him. I enjoyed every moment I got to spend with my dad, especially when it was on special trips like this.

Our journey to Trieste was uneventful. The wedding went on as planned. My grandparents, uncles, and aunts joined the plethora of noisy guests and I enjoyed my time with all of them. The merriment continued as everyone ate boiled eggs, radicchio and polenta and filled their cups with grappa. The guests joined in song as one man played his accordion. It was a very happy day for all, especially for me. Family is important and celebrations such as that one helped to instill this passion deeper into my being. To this day, there is nothing more important to me than family.

As the evening turned into night, Dad and I got on the bike and began our journey back to Udine – or at least that's what our plan was. On our way home, we had to cross Il Carso which was a chain of desolated and dry hills. Along with incredible views, these hills provided treacherous curves, tunnels and an assortment of rocks. As we approached Il Carso, we got a flat tire. Dad proceeded to pull over and patch the hole. It was repaired with the usual supplies, along with a long list of choice words that I could not understand.

Our trip continued for another few minutes before, low and behold, we got another flat. Dad became louder, which in turn allowed me to add a few more interesting words to my young vocabulary. He quickly patched the inner tube and we continued on our way – but not for long.

By now, the night had turned pitch-black and the tires continued to become flat. The more we attempted to get closer to home, the more flats we would get. Finally, Dad ran out of patches.

It was at this point in time that Dad had a brilliant idea which could revolutionize the tire industry. He could not understand why no one had thought of it before. He removed the inner tubes from the tires and threw them away. He then began the tedious task of filling the tires with pine needles. It not only was ingenious, but was a very resourceful idea. The road was lined with plenty of trees to provide us with the necessary materials to complete the task.

"HA", he triumphantly exclaimed "get flat now if you can!"

Unfortunately, but not unexpectedly, Dad's idea did not work. He pushed the bike for the last twenty kilometers of our journey. A trip that should have been a few hours ended up lasting all through the night.

We reached our destination at dawn. As we arrived, my dad took a short detour to the river, La Roia, which flowed directly across from the restaurant. With the last bit of strength left in him, he resolutely lifted the Triumph and tossed it into the river, then turned his back and walked home. No words were used this time. I don't think words were necessary.

Once we were home, Dad went directly to his room and remained there for a few hours. I carefully explained the night's events to my mom. She covered her mouth and quickly walked out to the back yard. There, she was free to laugh, away from my dad's radar.

The next day, it was business as usual. The restaurant opened and was soon filled with soldiers and GIs. My dad, however, was nowhere to be found.

Our apartment was directly above the restaurant. I looked out the window and could see Dad in the cold river. The water was up to his waist as he looked for his bike. All that could be heard was the sound of rushing water and a few more colorful words.

I went downstairs and told Mom what I had seen and she in turn told some soldiers. After much laughter was had by all, the men got up and proceeded outside to assist my dad in his task.

Later that day, the group of wet men sat drinking. The drinks were on the house, of course. There was laughter and further enhancement to my vocabulary, this time with English words, as the soldiers and my dad attempted to remove a great deal of leeches from their cold legs.

The following morning, we were greeted by a nice surprise next to the wet bike, courtesy of the GIs who had sacrificed their limbs to help us. Lying on the ground, we found brand new tires and inner tubes. The bike and tires worked great after that. We loved Dad's Triumph and we couldn't help but love those GIs. There was nothing they couldn't do and almost nothing they wouldn't do to help someone in need.

Thank you, GIs!

SAFARI

Udine, Italy

In early 1948, my parents made an announcement that would change our lives forever. They informed us that we were moving. This move would give our family a much needed new start, away from war-bruised Europe and all of the dark memories it held. My mind tried to wrap itself around the thought of moving out of Italy. Where would we go?

A big, resounding answer came from my father: Venezuela.

Venezuela? Was that what he said? If you have never heard of Venezuela, I suggest you do what I had to do and consult a world map or a grown-up. It is the northernmost country in South America, north of Brazil, east of Colombia, west of Guyana. Venezuela contains miles and miles of coastline along the Antilles Sea. Of course, this information is only helpful if you know where South America is. Little did my parents know that their big news would turn into a geography lesson.

As we gathered around Dad with our eyes wide-open to the possibilities, he explained that Venezuela is a tropical country. We would have no winters to deal with. The only two seasons of this Eden were wet and dry. The thought of not being cold again excited us. It would take a while to thaw our bones from the cold European winters, but we were ready and willing to give it a try. Dad's words still echo in my ears: "No more cold. It will be spring and summer with nothing in between!" It sounded divine!

The more I learned about our new home, the more my imagination ran wild. We would be near many islands surrounding Venezuela. These Caribbean Islands include Margarita, Cubagua, Isla de Coche, La Tortuga, La Orchila, Los Roques, and many more. Most of them were notorious pirate-infested islands in stories from long ago. My little mind couldn't handle the excitement of the danger and adventure awaiting us on those shores! What little boy doesn't get excited at the mention of pirates!

Dad continued with his description of our new home.

82

"The rainforest takes half of the territory and in it is the third largest river in South America, The Orinoco. The Andes Mountains are on the west side, and they run down to Chile and Argentina."

"Wait, Dad!" I interrupted. "Did you say 'The Andes'?"

I had been reading a book at school called "*Cuore*" (Heart). In one particular chapter, called "From the Apennines to the Andes," a young boy decided to go on a solo adventure to find his mother. She had gone to Argentina to try to find work and the boy longed to be reunited with her, so he traveled there by himself, making it a great story for any boy to read.

I was sold. Venezuela, I was coming for you!

From that day on, we would hear nightly bedtime stories about this wild land. Dad had never been there, but he imagined it as wild as the unexplored regions of Africa. He, too, would let his mind wander and we'd often find him deep in thought about his new life ahead. These stories would keep my brother and me on high alert, eyes wide-open in the dark of night as we listened to every word spoken.

One such story went a little something like this:

It was a very dark night and rain fell heavily as we set up camp in the deepest part of the uncharted jungle. The landscape was flat, with nothing but trees surrounding us in every direction. It was a rare cold night. We made a bonfire to keep us warm, but the real reason for this fire was to keep the wild beasts away. I informed our porters and helpers to come closer to the fire for warmth. Through the pitch-black darkness we heard roars of wild creatures. They poured out of animals such as jaguars, tigers, lions and black panthers and we could hear them coming closer to our camp. These big cats were afraid of fire, and my party was afraid of the big cats. This fire-cat relationship helped motivate everyone to keep the fire blazing throughout the night.

Take a moment now and picture how scared my eyes would have looked in our dark room. I hid my face under the covers, excited yet terrified of what he would say next. Dad continued his story with as much mystery as that of a gripping novel.

I was tired and since the others were awake, I decided to close my eyes for a while. I knew I should not fall asleep but I could not help it. Unfortunately, everyone was thinking the same thing. Soon, the entire camp was sound asleep and unaware of the approaching danger.

I was suddenly awakened by loud pops: POP, POP, POP! I was startled and for a moment, forgot where I was. Once I regained alertness, I noticed the popping noises were coming from the fire. I quickly got up and ran towards it and, to my horror, saw that the porters had laid their heads too close to the fire. The heat from the fire led to immense pressure build-up, causing their heads to pop like popcorn. Fortunately for them, thinking on my feet was my specialty. I grabbed each man by the feet and pulled them away from the fire. I then began to open every bottle of wine I could find and used the corks to plug the holes in their heads. It wasn't pretty, but it did the job.

I bet that you are now as eager and curious to hear how the story ends as I was that night. So without further delay, I give you the grand finale to this tale.

As I was busy plugging the injured heads of my party, I failed to notice the fire. It was slowly dying, becoming smaller and smaller, until not a spark remained. No fire meant the big cats would come. On came the headlamp and, to my horror, I saw the reflection of fangs and red eyes. There were too many to count and they were increasing in number by the minute. I quickly grabbed my gun and encouraged those around me who were feeling better to do the same. We began to fire without ceasing until the sun broke through in the morning sky. It was the largest confrontation ever recorded between man and beast.

As the sky started to brighten, the eyes we shot at began to disappear along with the roars that had plagued our ears all night. We had won the battle. Some of the porters were still complaining of headaches but we had all miraculously survived. As we prepared our early breakfast, I looked out at the surrounding landscape. I noticed large hills that had not been there the night before. I distinctly remembered being on flat land when we set up camp. It was then that I realized what I was looking at were not hills. They were piles and piles of the lions, tigers, jaguars and black panthers we had killed that night. I smiled to myself as I thought, "If it wasn't them, then those hills would have been us."

Of course, no child in his right mind would be able to sleep after a story like that. I was no exception. The following nights did not provide gentler tales of the land that would soon be our home. The nights became restless as I thought about what would be in store for me in Venezuela.

And I have my dad to thank for that.

A TRIP TO THE OTHER SIDE
OF THE POND

Genoa, Italy

It was a cold and gray December day in 1948 when our ship left Genoa, Italy, heading for Venezuela. On the other side of the Atlantic (aka "the Pond") was my eagerly awaiting dad who had left a few months prior to find us a home. We had said goodbye to Trieste and Udine, our home for so many years, for good. On our journey to Genoa, we toured cities such as Montebello Vicentino, Venice and Padua. It would be my last time in Italy and an ending to that chapter in my life.

We boarded the small, rusted old bucket called Il Lugano. With a very heavy heart, I hugged my grandparents for the last time. In tears, I thought about my school and childhood friends. I was about to leave them behind forever. I was eight years and eight months old. My little brother was too young to realize the permanency of our upcoming adventure.

Il Lugano's condition did not reassure me of its ability to cross "the Pond." The water was calm, yet it rolled from side to side as if in stormy waters. As a matter of fact, I went as far as to ask my mom if this particular ship had previously sunk and somehow been resurrected from the depth of the sea. Some passengers found my question child-like and funny, yet others wondered....

My premonition was right but the timing was a bit off. A few years later, I found that Il Lugano finally did sink near Sicily.

As we pulled out of the harbor, my mind switched slowly from sadness to excitement. I, a kid from Trieste, was crossing the Atlantic! A new life waited filled with new lands, new languages and the hope (and slight fear) that Dad's stories were not just stories.

We had managed to book a cabin in second-class. We shared this space with good people whose faces and genders I do not remember. I do, however, remember their smell. You never know what your mind will engrave in its ridges.

Once we settled into our cabin and adjusted our land legs to become true sea legs, the adventure of exploring began. It was a time filled with many firsts. For the first time I saw dolphins swimming along the ship, flying fish, darkly colored water, and entrancing foam as the ship navigated the long, rolling waves.

I felt privileged when I was informed that our meals would be served before third-class and after first-class and the ship's officers. I believe that there was also another class – a no class – without any rooms, just a large area where everyone spent their days and nights. I'm not quite sure when they ate.

Our dining tables were functional but strange-looking to a landlubber like me. They had unusual hinged rims that prevented dishes, cups and food from falling on the floor. The ship's movements made sure that these rims were an absolute necessity throughout the entire journey.

I, along with several other passengers, became seasick almost every day of our journey. The seas were merciless when it came to waves and the condition of our ship did not ease the matter in any way. Upon finding relief from my sickness, I would enjoy the time I had until the next bout of illness began. It was just something one learned to accept and I did not let this hinder my excitement. There was much to keep me occupied.

I only remember two children in our section: a brother and sister. They were Cuban and despite our language barrier, we had no problem communicating. Children have this uncanny ability to make friends wherever they go, regardless of the situation. They called me *burro,* Spanish for donkey. I took little offense in this since *burro* meant butter in Italian. What's more delicious than fresh butter? I took it as a compliment.

Occasionally and depending on the weather, a big white canvas was hung outside on the ship and a movie was projected. This was the same movie, repeated time and time again. We didn't mind. It kept us entertained enough to forget how sick we felt and how long our journey was. Watching it over and over again helped us get the timing right for when to cheer or boo. By the time we arrived, we had it down to a science.

Our first stop on *terra firma* was Barcelona, Spain. While some went into town to do a quick tour of this historic city, others stayed on the ship. We were one of those lucky few admiring this city from the decks of the rusty old bucket.

Once we crossed the Rock of Gibraltar, we began our long navigation through the open ocean. For the next two to three days, we would not see any coastlines. Our sights consisted of water and long rolling waves, leading to more bouts of seasickness.

Our next stop was at Tenerife on the Canary Islands. This was not far from Spain and across Morocco. There, my excitement exploded when I was told that El Teide, the local volcano, was fuming. The promise of seeing such a sight made me so giddy that I nearly drove my mom crazy. Regardless of how hard I looked and much to my disappointment, I saw neither smoke nor lava.

The next day at port proved to be much better than the day before. Not only was it warmer and the sun brighter, but we were able to tour the city. This is where I sampled bananas for the first time in my life. The smell and flavor would be something I would never forget. They tasted as sweet as they smelled and with every bite I felt that I was one step closer to our new home. I wondered how many bunches my dad would have waiting for me. They were the best bananas I would ever have!

While the banana was exciting, nothing would prepare me for what I saw next. Right there, in front of my little eyes, was a camel! Life here was diverse. It was exciting to hear Spanish and to see people with different skin colors than mine. I found life's variety wonderful and marvelous. I was very reluctant when night came and we headed back to Il Lugano. I certainly did not want this day to end.

The next day brought another surprise shortly before departing. Just after breakfast, some passengers began tossing coins into the water. Mom hurried me so that I could watch the local children dive after the coins. I could not believe my eyes! The water was so clear I could see the glistening coins reflecting as though they were little mirrors sinking deeper and deeper. I was in awe as I watched the kids going after them. The Canary Islands did not disappoint!

We soon departed that part of the world. The long leg of our journey would take more than two weeks, offering no land in sight. Seagulls no longer flew over us and the waves made me wonder about the possibility of capsizing. Through our small window, I could see the scenery change from blue skies to underwater in a split second. There were a few storms, remarkable enough to remember, that washed out the ship. We suffered through them but got our reward in the form of beautiful rainbows. The open ocean offered unobstructed views of these colorful wonders.

Our nights were filled with all kinds of time-passing music. Some nights included dancing, while others were a more simple session of accordion, guitar and singing. Italian songs echoed the halls, the most popular being *Santa Lucia* and *Torna a Surriento*. Looking back, I see how special it was to see people of diverse backgrounds coming together to have a good time.

After what seemed like a never-ending number of days, we reached our destination: the port of Puerto Cabello in Venezuela. The weather was warm. In fact, it was warmer than anything I had felt my entire life! The water was choppy and the breeze was pleasant on my face. The coastline was lined with rows upon rows of palms, patched with dark green coconut and mango trees.

Immediately, I noticed how different the pier was to the grand European piers of Genoa or Tenerife. It was small and contained none of the familiar large cranes I had grown accustomed to. As we got closer, I watched the crews on both land and ship prepare to moor and secure the beast that carried us over the

Atlantic. Even though we had stopped moving and were securely moored the ship continued to roll from side to side, as if waving us goodbye.

The unloading of luggage began. Some passengers had brought many of their possessions from the old world, including furniture. Fortunately for the small pier, the ship had its own crane and used it to carefully lower the precious cargo to the anxiously waiting owners. Each item was lowered using heavy cargo nets. Watching from the deck, I squinted as I attempted to distinguish our belongings – two heavy trunks and some old luggage.

We waited patiently until the announcement to disembark came. With our documents and travel bags in hand, we walked down the long plank that had been lowered off the side of the ship. I noticed a second plank had been lowered but was limited to strong, shirtless and shoeless men whose primary task was to carry heavy belongings for passengers. Much to my amusement, I was privileged enough to witness one of these strong lads with a heavy bag on his head, fall off the plank and into the warm, tropical water. I probably laughed louder than I should have but no one seemed to mind.

We quickly spotted Dad and his friend. It was a relief and joy to see him, knowing that I barely escaped death in the decrepit and rusty Il Lugano. As I stepped onto firm ground, I felt that it too was moving. I wasn't sure if the ground could move or if I was just dizzy from weeks at sea. That didn't stop me from what I needed to do next.

I ran straight to my dad who was all smiles. My little legs could go no faster as I ran to the man who had made this adventure possible. Before he took me into his strong embrace, Dad gave me a gift I will never forget: A very real, vividly green, yellow and red parrot! My own jungle creature!

This was a powerful moment of realization. The moment I knew, without a doubt, that Dad's stories were real after all.

Part 2:
Venezuela

THE FIRST DAY

Puerto Cabello, Venezuela

There is a first day for everything: first day of life, first day of school, first day driving, first day on the job, and so forth. This first day was just as meaningful.

My imagination had already been stimulated before leaving Italy by the endless stories my father told of our new homeland. I looked around and absorbed every inch of scenery: trees, birds, and colorful houses. All around me were people from all parts of the world. I saw kids my own age, playing shirtless and barefoot. Everything was a complete contrast to the gray, dull colors of the post-war Italy we left behind. The landscape of lush plants and colorful flowers consumed my overflowing brain. With every turn, my mind conceived a new adventure I was sure to have. I was convinced that I was in one of those Tarzan movies Dad loved so much.

Lunchtime came soon after disembarking but I wasn't sure I was hungry. My palate was accustomed to my dad's restaurant and Italian cuisine, so I was hesitant about the eatery my parents decided upon.

The restaurant was in an old colonial house painted a faded orange and blue. The outer walls were weathered and peeling, revealing the clay used in its construction. The entrance door had a curtain made of plastic pearls which helped prevent flies and other bugs from entering the restaurant. All the tables and chairs were rustic, there was no wine, and none of the waiters wore white aprons or black pants like my dad used to wear. The plates they brought to our table did not contain the usual polenta, pasta and radicchio. Instead, they were covered with black beans, strips of beef and fried plantains. I was offered bananas, mangoes, and guavas, all of them very different from the customary apples, grapes, peaches, and mulberries of Italy. I chose to eat a banana due to my previous experience with them. Other than that, I had convinced myself that I would just have to go hungry.

I was overwhelmed with the black and white difference of this land. Nothing felt familiar but despite my resolution, I was eventually persuaded to break my vow. I gave in to the deliciousness of a tempting bowl of Sancocho (a heavy soup with beef, chicken, corn, tapioca, potatoes, and cilantro). It was worth every bite.

Although nothing was familiar, there was one thing that instantly caught my interest: soda. The sugary, bubbly deliciousness of a cold bottle of Coca-Cola made me think, just for a minute, that I had been living under a rock. How could I have survived without drinking this until now? What other little secrets did this upside-down world hold?

My lack of familiarity caused me to doubt where we were for the first time since our adventure began. Were we really in South America or on a different planet? It wouldn't have surprised me if Tarzan himself had popped in and sat next to me at the table. The best part was that the day was not over yet!

After our lunch escapade, the long trip home to Caracas began. The winding roads proved to be too much for my already sensitive stomach, whose contents ended up on all kinds of trees and bushes. Eventually, I settled into my seat and watched the houses go by. Tall green blades of grass grew on the roof tops of the houses as pigs and chickens went in and out their front doors like any family member would.

Every few kilometers, our car was stopped at check points called Alcabalas. Our papers were checked and we were asked to step out of the car and walk over crudely-cut fabric pieces soaked in chemicals. This cleaning of shoes and feet was an effective method used to stop the spread of Foot-and-Mouth disease that was plaguing the area. I followed the adults' lead without question and we were soon back on our way.

The winding road from the port at Puerto Cabello climbed higher and higher, leaving coconut palms and other lowland vegetation behind. The higher we climbed the darker, thicker, and greener it became. The abundance of mango, papaya and avocado trees was overwhelming as we reached the proximity of Las Trincheras. Immediately upon our arrival, the road changed to a less serpent-like travel, allowing my restless stomach to settle a bit more. As we approached El Lago de Valencia and Maracay, I could see fields upon fields of sugar canes surrounded by mango trees. It's amazing how much the landscape changed with every turn. I gave up on expecting any type of consistency and decided to just sit back and enjoy the ride.

We took a short break after several hours of travel at an historical landmark called El Samán de Güere. This was an enormous tree under which Simon Bolivar, the historic liberator of Venezuela, and his followers had taken an extended rest during the fight for freedom during the early 1800s. The tree was already quite old and was showing serious signs of its age. I couldn't get too close it because it was surrounded by a fence. There was a large statue of

El Libertador, along with a plaque commemorating the freedom of the Venezuelan people from the tyranny of Spain on July 5, 1811.

After our sight-seeing, we continued on what seemed like a never-ending trip to the capital city of Caracas. The scenery was breathtaking but nothing was prettier to me than the parrot I held. My new best friend was all that mattered to me. I imagined all the fun the two of us would have as soon as I could teach him some Italian.

Our first view of Caracas was the area called El Paraiso. I was shocked to see so many tall trees within the city itself. The streets were nothing like the narrow roads in the crowded cities of Italy. These were wide enough to allow two buses, a few bikes and horse pulled carts to pass at the same time! The cars themselves were enormous in size compared to the Italian Topolino and scooters I was accustomed to seeing. I was pretty sure the fertile tropical environment made everything bigger.

It was a relief to find the city temperature to be spring-like, compared to the hot, tropical weather we had experienced during our journey. It was perfect, just like Dad said it would be. I could hardly believe my luck and I couldn't stop thanking him for the opportunity.

For the first few days, we stayed with some family friends. They had a son my age who became an instant friend to me. It helped that he was able to speak Italian and not that foreign Spanish all the other kids around us spoke. It gave me a bit of comfort and familiarity. We would spend hours taking turns riding his bike and exploring our surroundings.

Soon enough, the time came when we would move to our own home, located in La Subida de Catia, near El Junquito. It was a little cinder block house with a noisy metal roof, making it nearly impossible to talk during a strong rain storm. The front yard had a little fence with only a couple of acacia-type shrubs. The flooring in the house consisted of dirt, which I guess would be good if you hated to sweep. Our tiny backyard contained a fresh water tank and an outhouse. As far as furniture, the only pieces I remember where the two cots my little brother and I slept in. I knew things would be okay when I laid my eyes upon those cots. Sleep was very important to me because exploring took a lot of energy and I planned on doing a lot of it.

Eventually, we settled into our new life. Dad had picked up some Spanish during the time he had been here and was immediately promoted to "family interpreter". Mom, my brother and I only knew a few words: *burro* (Spanish for donkey, Italian for butter) and *cambures* (bananas). That was enough for me. I was too busy waiting for another adventure to begin to worry about learning Spanish. Lucky for me, I wouldn't have to wait too long before that adventure came my way.

STARS AND SPARKS

Caracas, Venezuela

A few months into our new life, Venezuela continued to be a mysterious land to us all. This tropical paradise had everything my Tarzan-wannabe dad could have desired: endless beaches and fish supply, unexplored rainforest with limitless hunting game, the high Andes Mountains containing some snow caps, rivers full of piranhas and caimans, and the deep and unexplored caves of La Cueva del Guácharo. Of course, the most awe-inspiring and breathtaking of all was (and still is) Angel Falls, the tallest waterfall in the world. Every corner of this country contained a new discovery.

Not long after our arrival, Dad came home with a couple of wild turkeys. He was an exceptional marksman with many weapons, in this case a slingshot. His aim was admirable, allowing him to always bring home the bacon; but in our case, it was usually bacon-substitute. Being the good hunter and provider that he was, Dad plucked the dark feathers, cleaned and gutted the turkey and gave it to Mom to prepare for dinner. My mom always worked her magic with whatever food my dad brought home and this was no exception.

Because we didn't have much money, these turkeys became an important part of our diet. They were in large supply and relatively easy to catch. The only difficulty was they tended to fly around in circles at high altitudes. This delayed the capturing process because my dad would have to wait until they landed, which often happened to be close to some dead critter. He had to aim so that the turkey would fall away from the decaying animals.

For almost an entire week we dined on this turkey delicacy, until the day we received a knock on the door. It was the local police.

"Sir," the officer gravely stated, "you have been killing protected birds. Please come with us to the police station for some questioning." We understood enough Spanish to see they meant business so we followed them.

We reached the station not knowing why we were being brought in. It took a few minutes of talking, signing and pointing for us to understand what they were trying to say. Apparently, the wild turkeys were protected because they ate dead animals, helping to keep diseases under control. Our "turkeys" were vultures.

Upon learning this little detail, we all began to vomit. It was quite a sight. Fortunately for us, this amused the police and helped them understand our mistake. We weren't arrested but instead allowed to return home to recuperate from our unfortunate error. We gave them something to laugh about for weeks. In time, we would become well acquainted with the police due to other misunderstandings, but that's a different story.

Once home, Dad thought it would be safer if we were to learn a bit more about the Venezuelan fauna. We decided to turn our attention over to fishing. Next time, we would obtain our free food from the sea. What could go wrong?

Our next problem with catching our food came the following weekend at a remote beach called Macuto in the northern Venezuelan coast, about one and a half hours from home depending on traffic.

It was a dark night with no moon in sight. The ocean waves were relatively calm based on local standards, and rain fell from the clouds. The temperature was cool which helped create an eerie environment. I was one scared, cold and soaked little boy, but willing to follow my dad wherever he went.

Dad, a sort of Jungle Jim with a dash of Superman mixed in, did not own a boat during this time. Owning a boat would have allowed us to deploy our long and heavy fishing net with ease. Dad wanted a boat but we had not been in Venezuela long enough to have saved sufficient money to purchase one. Our only choice was to follow Dad's motto: When you don't have a boat, you swim!

Swimming was exactly what he did. He tied one end of the net to a heavy rock conveniently placed on the beach. He then placed the other end around his chest and over one shoulder and proceeded to swim in a large circle towards the other end of the beach. He was particularly good at finding solutions.

After Dad came out of the water, he tied his end of the net and we waited. This allowed enough time for our victims to get caught in our trap. My mouth watered at the thought of what mom would make with our catch. At least this time, I was sure it would be something safe to eat.

Soon, Dad began the long process of pulling the entire net back to the shore. Normally, this type of tedious operation would require the strength of several men, but all we needed was a man like my dad. He waded out a bit, ignoring the fact that a dark night at sea usually meant that barracudas, sharks, eels, rays and the like could possibly cross his path.

Dad lit a lantern and as he pulled the net in, I could see silvery flashes of light reflecting off the trapped fish. I patiently sat waiting while he remained busy with the catch. I wasn't scared anymore, and soon found myself beginning to dose off. Just as I closed my eyes for a little rest, I heard Dad call out to me.

"Hey!" he shouted. "Come here! I need your help with this fish."

I snapped out of it. Me? What? I had never seen a live fish before. They were usually dead, gutted and cooked by the time they crossed my path. Why would he need me?

"Who, me?" I said, playing dumb.

"Yes. Who else? Grab that one fish for me."

I trotted over to the water and looked to where he pointed. That "fish" was not what I had imagined a live fish would look like. It was shaped funny: flat and round at the same time. It was extremely large, ugly, slimy, mean looking and full of grunting noises. I refused to grab it. It scared me!

After Dad called me a few choice names, I became more concerned about him than the fish so I went for it. My small hand trembled as I reached out to touch the slimy thing with my little index finger.

You know that feeling you get when lightning flashes and scares you enough to jump? Take that feeling, multiply it by one hundred, add electricity to it and then you might be able to sympathize with what I felt next. The instant my fingertip touched the fish, I leapt in the air and my brain burst in flashes of beautiful stars and sparks as a powerful electric shock ran through my entire wet body.

A few seconds passed before I came around enough to find the entire situation more amusing than painful. As I sat there recuperating, I heard my dad speak.

"Did you have fun? Next time you see a fish like that, you will know better than to touch it. I, too, got an electric shock and wanted to share this experience with you. Now, you are wiser."

That was my introduction to the electric ray, The Torpedo! I learned two powerful lessons that night.

First, don't touch electric rays.

Second, always proceed with caution when Dad asks you to do something, because it usually means there is a lesson he wants you to learn.

Once again, thank you, Dad!

FROGS

Lago de Valencia, Venezuela

During the golden time of the 1940s, Venezuela's natural beauty was at its prime. Big cities had not taken over the land, so nature was still in control. One place in particular, El Lago de Valencia, was a beautiful, large and wild lake about two miles from the city of Maracay. The kings and rulers of these parts were both caimans and the baba, their smaller relative. Their minions included piranhas, guabina fish and payaras (also known as Vampire Fish). If you have never seen some of these animals, I highly recommend you do an Internet search in order to fully understand how amazingly dangerous these waters were.

Living in the same area as these beasts were beautiful birds such as red and white ibis, cranes, anhingas, parrots and macaws. Roaming the land and waters were anacondas, a plethora of snakes, pecari, deer and numerous other mammals. There were more critters than I could count. Last but not least out of all these were the mosquitoes, ticks and venomous spiders that truly helped make this lake a tropical paradise indeed! In order for me to explain the large amount of tropical flora, I would require the assistance of explorers such as Humboldt, Pittier and many others who are more versed in the matter.

If you were to look up this lake now, you would find it completely changed as the thirsty cities expanded and the industrial complexes sucked much of the lake's water. In the early 60s, the lake had already shrunk considerably and by the time the 1970s rolled along, the city of Maracay had expanded a half a mile over where the water used to be.

But I digress.

My first visit to the lake was in the early 50s after one of Dad's bright ideas. He loved frog legs and would go to extremes to get them into his hands. He heard the lake was the place to go for this beloved delicacy, so off we went.

We packed our car to the brim with much needed supplies: a large number of hooks, wine, tridents, wine, ice, wine, a shot gun, wine, a few friends, wine, a large aluminum boat, and just in case we ran out, some more wine. My packing list, on the other hand, was rather short. I just made sure to bring myself.

In Italy, Dad the hunter was accustomed to going on

frog hunts at night so he decided this time would not be any different. We left at dusk on a trip that would be between three to four hours long, depending on how many stops they would have to make for me. There were no public bathrooms back then. You either took your chance at coming face to face with a jaguar or wet your pants. I didn't mind the risk because after all, my dad was Super Dad and in my mind he was invincible!

Upon arriving, Dad and his friends put the boat into the swampy water. Without the modern conveniences of paved parking lots and boat launch ramps, our way of getting into the water involved mud and more water. The lake was surrounded by a swamp filled with water lilies, tall grass and all the critters we discussed above. Food always tastes better when you have to work hard to get it.

Once the boat was loaded, the men began to push it through the mud and tall grass. I didn't understand it then, but now I see that the swamp itself was punishing them.

I did not feel any of the same sensations the men in the water felt. Because I was young, I sat comfortably in the boat, enjoying the ride and the little bit of the scenery I could see in the darkness of night. My jobs were easy: to hold the kerosene lamp so everyone could see, and to slap mosquitoes. One of those jobs was much easier than the other.

Eventually, we reached the safety of deeper waters. The men helped each other climb into the boat and quickly grabbed an oar. Their strength was clearly evident when they began to row. I could feel the breeze move my hair as the boat glided with ease across the dark, murky waters of the lake.

It wasn't long after they began rowing that we suddenly discovered the cause of the swamp's wrath. Leeches were on everyone who had pushed the boat through the water. The sight of three grown men stripping in the moonlight while trying not to rock the boat into the leech-infested water was only made funnier by them plucking leeches off each other's bodies. It was quite a show, and I was grateful to be the one watching and not the one performing.

Soon after the leech fiasco, a good mood was re-established thanks to the consumption of a generous quantity of wine. The leeches were either dead or back in the water and all the articles of clothing were back were they belonged. There was plenty of laughter and everyone soon settled back into the boat, returning to the task at hand. Four pairs of eyes began scanning the dark water for frogs.

Unlike the noisy entrance we had made, we soon kicked across the lake in stealth mode. Our boat moved slowly while the men paddled gently, avoiding any unnecessary noise. The calm was relaxing. I sat back and took in the sights as the reflecting moon lit our way.

Patience was key during our hunt and despite the rocky start, everyone remained committed to finding these frogs. Excitement built as someone spotted the first pair of eyes and in no time at all, the lake seemed to be covered with them. I was eager at the thought of a big, heaping plate of frog legs for lunch. I was surprised to notice that the eyes were red. While I couldn't recall what color frog's eyes were, what truly caught my attention was the alarmingly large size of said eyes. Common sense told me that the frogs belonging to them must be immensely larger than I was accustomed to. I knew that dinner would definitely be filling and more satisfying than our previous "wild turkey" feast. I questioned Dad about the enormity of the eyes we were seeing and he assured me that in the tropical jungles, frogs could be quite massive. That was the icing on the cake for me. I would soon be in frog leg heaven.

Still using our covert movements, we approached a pair of eyes. Dad gently placed the net in the water in preparation to "scoop" the frog up. It was a good, sturdy net used mainly for catching trout. When we were closer, he swung the net over the eyes in order to catch the frog if it tried to jump. To everyone's surprise, the net bounced back into the air with a loud thump as it hit the top of a five-foot long man-eating caiman's head.

Dad turned to us, his bulging eyes saying it all: no frogs today, only caimans.

Not finding frogs did not hinder my dad's sense of adventure. The men decided if they couldn't bring frogs home, they would bring caimans. Bravely reaching into the water, one of men grabbed the caiman by the tail and with all his strength jerked him into the boat. He was a big, strong man but soon found that taming a caiman inside an aluminum boat with three other people on board was

113

unexpectedly challenging. The caiman whipped its tail and snapped its powerful jaws at every movement, causing quite an uproar as men scrambled for safety while trying not to upset the small aluminum boat.

Panic began to set until Dad suddenly remembered that one of the boat's seats opened up like a chest. This saved us all from having to leap into the caiman and leech infested waters to seek relative safety. The men all ganged up on the caiman and were able to launch him into the holding container. It was decided that the biggest of the men would sit on the lid so that the caiman couldn't get out. This was a good solution, but made the man sitting on the lid jump out of his skin every time the caiman moved. He found it much harder than anticipated keeping that beast under control. I learned never to underestimate what these powerful creatures can do.

Many would think this would be enough action for one night but then again, my dad had an unconventional idea of adventure. The hunt continued. Since the one and only holding spot was occupied, they decided it would be much easier to deal with a dead caiman than another live one. The men grabbed another caiman out of the water and shot it in the head. On and on this went, battling the caimans until they lay dead at the bottom of our boat. We captured five more caimans by the time we decided to call it a night. The live one remained in the chest, occasionally lashing out in its outrage at being contained.

We returned to shore with a heavy boat and

exhausted men. The weight of the boat made it absolutely necessary to jump back in the water in order to push it through the muddy swamp near the shore, leading me to be exposed to yet another bout of angry, cursing, and naked men desperately attempting to remove leeches. It was like Christmas all over again.

Leeches gone and clothes back on, Dad and companions loaded the five dead caimans into the trunk, and then wrestled the live one in as well. I observed all the happenings from the safety and comfort of the car. As we pulled onto the road, the commotion in the trunk grew louder and louder. Apparently, the live caiman still had fight in him. Dad stopped the car and all three men got out. From my seat I could hear the mumbling of their voices, the trunk opening, and few smacking sounds followed by complete silence. No more noises came from the trunk and we drove straight for home. We were beat, but proud to be bringing home such a wonderful surprise.

Dad suddenly had a brilliant realization. He recalled that caiman skins sold for quite a bit of money. A plan was made that once they got home, the caimans would be placed in one of the courtyards and skinned.

*Side note: Our living quarters were located in a very popular "barrio" called La Pastora. We lived in a large colonial style house as boarders who were renting a room. Our rent not only included the use of our room, but dinner every night as well as the use of a common bathroom. These houses were made out of bricks with two courtyards: one would function as a common room, serving mostly for entertainment, and was usually covered. The second courtyard was larger and was connected to the kitchen, bathroom and a large containment unit filled with tap water. Needless to say, this second courtyard where the caimans were to be placed was common ground as well.

The next day, the caimans were skinned and hung up to dry on the community clothes lines across the courtyard. My dad was always good at finding new uses for everyday items.

I must profess that none of the men were professionals at skinning large reptiles. Undaunted, they proceeded with their plan. Their inexperience was clearly evident by the lack of crucial steps in their procedure, particularly when they failed to clean all the flesh from the skin and neglected to salt it. These seemingly little things would later lead to huge consequences.

The weather following the skinning was very warm and humid. This, in turn, produced a foul, gut-wrenching stench that could be enjoyed not only by everyone in our entire building, but also by anyone who unwittingly happened to step out of their home in our surrounding neighborhood.

Two malodorous days passed.

On the third day, and after our neighbors had suffered enough, there was a knock on our door. Our room became as silent as a tomb. Dad sat still, refusing to move. He knew something had gone terribly wrong and was afraid of what was waiting for him on the other side. My mom, being the strong woman that she was, stood up and opened the door for him.

The room was immediately filled with policemen wanting to know where we were keeping the corpses. It took a while to calm them down and be able explain what the actual smell was. Once realizing we didn't have a plethora of dead human bodies in our room but instead half a dozen dead caimans in the courtyard, the officers ordered Dad to get rid of any and all signs of the animals.

To this day, I still don't know if the money my dad paid the policemen was for a "smell and illegal caiman skinning" fine or something else… life was never dull at our house. As much as Mom wanted normalcy, this was our normal.

Thanks, Dad, for yet another page in my book.

A FRIEND NO MORE

Santa Lucia, Venezuela

For the most part, I was a typical eleven-year-old kid. The most noticeable difference between me and my friends was that I was afraid of my own shadow. Any little thing would send me off into fits of panic. Fortunately, I had the strongest, bravest and fiercest dad any kid could ask for. I know I have said before but I will never tire of saying it: my dad was Super Dad. No one could ever call him a coward; he was never afraid and he always took care of me. Always.

During this time of my life Super Dad had a brilliant idea: he would send me to spend a few days at his friend's hacienda. I can't remember his name, so I will call him Guido. Guido's house was located not far from the Venezuelan capital of Caracas were we lived. Staying with Guido would be yet another exciting adventure I would set out to conquer. I had been in Venezuela for several years now and I still couldn't get over the excitement this land constantly provided. There was always somewhere to go and something to do. Super Dad made sure of that.

I loved that hacienda, mostly because it was located in a chain of hills covered with more than enough wilderness to be called a jungle. It was a great place for deer, big cats, rabbits, snakes, and numerous other critters. The best part was the noticeably reduced number of ticks in the vicinity. It was the ideal location for outdoor exploration.

From the moment I arrived, I wanted to go night-hunting with my new headlamp and sixteen-gauge one-barrel shotgun. That being said, just because I wanted to go hunting did not mean I was brave enough to step foot outside the front door by myself. I begged Guido to take me. I craved the chance to be in the jungle. I knew Tarzan was in my blood and to this day, I believe my dad was related to him.

Although my desire was to go into the jungle, I spent most of that first day doing typical hacienda things. I rode a donkey, a horse, climbed a tree and ran around until I tired. I continued in my quest of convincing Guido to take me on the adventure I desired. Eventually, he reluctantly agreed. I had gotten my way but little did I know what this would mean.

As night fell, we gathered our equipment and headed out. We spent our time trying to find the trail of any animal. We walked in every direction with the hope of finding something to hunt. Three hours yielded nothing as we came to the realization that our outing was coming up short. Guido called it a night and we headed back to the house. Disappointment loomed over me.

As we approached the safety of the hacienda, I immediately spotted a pair of big, bright glowing eyes. There it was: my prey for the evening! There was no question in my mind. It began moving toward us at a rather fast pace. I saw the eyes coming closer and closer to where we stood. My instincts told me that I would be dinner for whatever big beast was galloping toward me. Guido was busy looking in a different direction. I knew this would be the night I would become a man. I would save us both!

I quickly grabbed my gun, took aim and shot right between the two glowing eyes.

It's amazing how our ears work. They can hear so many different sounds at the same time. On this particular night, I could clearly hear three sounds simultaneously: the BOOM of my gun, Guido shouting "NOOOOO!" and a pain-filled howl. I couldn't quite figure out how those sounds fit together but fortunately for me, Guido's actions and words soon explained it all.

I did not turn out to be the hero I was sure I would be that day. On the contrary, I had made Guido very angry.

Those galloping eyes were not the eyes of a beast of the wild running to devour us. No. Those eyes were running towards us to welcome us home. Those eyes belonged to Guido's best prized hunting dog.

Fortunately for everyone, especially the dog, I was a lousy shot. He would survive and live a long and happy life. I, on the other hand, was no longer welcome at the hacienda. Guido washed his hands of our family and we would never see him again. The incident was reason enough for him to rid himself of this pestering night-hunting eleven year-old.

I bet you are wondering if my courage improved. Did this adventure make me a man? Did facing an unknown danger shake me out of my childish fears? I will answer you honestly with a nice, resonating NO. Thanks for asking.

HARD LANDING

Caracas, Venezuela

Ah, the ripe age of fifteen. It is around this time when most kids, boys in particular, start to believe they are invincible. They begin to think all the disasters they had been taught to avoid were only legends told by anxious mothers. The wires in their heads get crossed and very bad ideas start to sound like brilliant rocket science. On this particular day in 1955, things weren't any different.

At this time in my life, I found great joy in swimming and was part of a local swim team. We were a bunch of young guys, fourteen of us, eager to be the best swimmers and divers in the entire country. Some succeeded, and others, like me, did not. I had an impeccable personal record, broken by none. I came in last every single time. If there were five competitors, I would have come in sixth. I was the one everyone could count on to make sure that "no man was left behind." Good old reliable me.

As I have mentioned before, Caracas is a very pleasant city. The average temperature is almost always between summer-time and spring-time. This particular day was no different from any other. The Olympic-sized pool in which we practiced was the only one of its kind in Caracas. It was part of private club in the center of the city on a prime lot located on Andrés Bello Avenue. It was the place to be if you wanted to play tennis, swim, dive, and socialize.

We had been practicing hard one day, but we grew tired of simply swimming back and forth under the stern direction of our coach. We wanted to play and have fun but couldn't do so while our coach was around. Fortunately for us, he decided it was time to leave as evening wrapped itself around the city. He grabbed his belongings promising that he would not be as easy on us during our next practice. This was followed by a communal groan.

Not long after our coach left, we decided that we needed to unwind with a nice game of swim tag. Fourteen rambunctious boys splashed around, enjoying our coach-free time for a while before deciding on diving. As the night progressed, the dives became more daring. Most of our maneuvers didn't have an official diving name. We just made them up as we went, always trying to outdo each other.

Through the laughter, I heard one of the guys call out for our attention. When we turned to him, we saw that he had removed his swim trunks and was now using it as a hat. We thought he was brilliant! It was a perfect time to start a good old fashioned game of follow-the-leader. Soon, nearly all the boys had new "hats" on as we continued our death-defying diving. I was too shy to undress but that didn't hinder my fun. Our merriment gradually grew in volume and we failed to realize that making too much noise was unwise.

On that particular evening, the club manager was busy touring the property with a potential new family. Our cheers of joy called his attention, and upon turning on the pool lights, he nearly fainted. It was a scandal. We were quickly escorted out and banned from any further unsupervised night swimming. The manager began locking the dressing room door in order to enforce his strict new policy. Word of the disgraceful incident quickly spread across our conservative town and we were marked as trouble makers.

That night sealed our fate... or so you would think.

Telling a child they can't do something will only make that child want to do it more. It's a simple and well known scientific fact and as true as Newton's Law of Gravity. The banning triggered the creative juices in our still-developing brains to flow.

Brainstorming sessions were called and ideas were presented on how we could regain access to the dressing rooms. Times were different then. We couldn't walk around town wearing our swimming trunks like some do now. It was not considered proper, and while propriety was not at the top of our list, we knew it would be a sure way to get caught. Days passed before a light bulb illuminated the idea of a lifetime.

The clubhouse building was adjacent to the local bowling alley. Conveniently, the roof had an opening which led directly into the bowling alley attic. This would be our new dressing room; it was an answer to our unruly prayers. We scaled up to the roof, snuck into the attic and changed into our swimming trunks. The distance to the pool was minimal, making this plan ideal.

Only a few chose to take the initial risk. I was not one of them. Our last incident left me a bit leery about trying a new stunt so I chose to let the others test the situation.

At this point in my story, I should describe the architecture of the time. Buildings during the 1950s in Venezuela were not made in the same manner as they are today. Instead of trusses and beams, the ceilings were supported by canes similar to those of sugar. They did their job, but were not meant to carry the burden of weight. A stroll in the attic of a building was no safe caper.

But what the heck, we were not engineers. A few kids stepped into the attic and began the laborious

126

task of changing into their swim trunks. After a few minutes of nothing happening, a few more entered. Soon enough, we were quietly swimming in the dark pool waters, wearing our hats. Everything went smoothly for a few weeks… until one particular Saturday night.

Our success had been shared with the rest of the swim team and it was only natural that they should join us in our night-swimming, hat-wearing ritual. The bowling alley, named Casablanca, was crowded with families and groups of friends. It was, after all, a weekend and there was much fun to be had.

All fourteen of us climbed the building using our stealthiest moves and no one inside was the wiser. In our excitement of having the whole gang together, we failed to remember to check how many of us were in our attic-turned-changing-room. As always, I stayed behind, choosing to change alone. Something told me not to go yet, and this night proved that my gut was to be trusted.

As quick as the flight of a humming bird, the ceiling cracked and slowly began to collapse under the weight of the boys. I could hear cracking and shouting as naked boys fell, one by one, into the crowded bowling alley. It was one of those moments that appear to be in slow motion. One boy would fall as another stood frozen, looking at him in shock until he, too, fell, creating a domino effect. One managed to hang on for dear life as the rest fell naked.

Because I was still on the roof, I wasn't able to see most of the chaos that followed. I could hear the cacophony coming from inside and my ears had to do the work of creating a picture of what I could not see. There was plenty of shouting mixed with screams of fear, cursing and contagious laughter. I found out later that some of those screams were coming from women who fainted at the sight of naked boys falling from the ceiling. I could hear a few panicked shouts wailing, "He's dead!" It was chaotic. It was funny. It was scary. It was everything all at once.

After all the panic, the comedic part of the fiasco became very apparent to everyone there. The scene in the bowling alley was unforgettable and would be spoken of for years to come. Some of the boys were taken into custody by the police. They were soon released, mostly because the bowling alley patrons were in a very good mood.

But out of the madness and chaos came a hero. Only one boy had remained lying in one of the lanes. He had not tried to run away like the others. He pretended to be knocked out. He was taken to the hospital and upon examination, released with no injuries. He, my friend, was our hero! He had laid there, in all his glory, accepting whatever retribution would come his way.

I'm sorry, but I am unable to give names of those involved. Most of these boys grew up to be very important government workers. They held such positions as Secretary of State and Secretary of Education. I can, however, tell you that it was Julio who had the idea. I don't know what happened to Julio and whether or not he's still alive, but thanks to him, I have this story to tell.

THE DRESSING ROOM

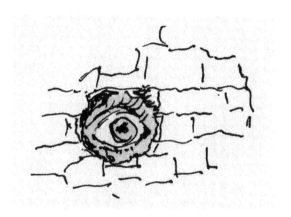

Caracas, Venezuela

I often felt sorry for the pool manager at the club. The gang and I seemed to gain great pleasure out of making his life miserable. He was constantly on guard and had a stress-induced twitch in his eye. If we weren't sneaking into the pool at night, we would be finding some other way to break the pool rules. I'm sure the only thing that kept him going was the vengeful aspiration of one day being able to catch us.

The pool dressing room was a small, short building consisting only of a boys' and a girls' dressing rooms next to each other. Above each dressing room door was a window just big enough to let air in and steam out. It wasn't much to look at but it had its function.

I was the youngest of the gang and I'm sure that was one of the reasons I was so shy. I would always patiently wait for the room to empty before changing. Thankfully, none of the boys teased me about it. Not because they were being nice, but rather they were busy with other things. While I waited my turn, I could see them gathered closely together, their faces pressed up against the wall. They would take turns, often leading to a shoving-match if one of them became impatient.

One afternoon, after waiting a long time, I found myself alone and began the task of changing out of the wet bathing suit. I always skipped the shower in order to avoid any potentially embarrassing incidents. As I finished my task, I noticed a small wad of newspaper shoved into a hole in the wall. It looked to me as if someone was using it as a plug of some sort. Curiosity got the better of me and I removed the newspaper, careful not to tear in any further. Low and behold, I had a clear view directly into the girls' dressing room. I took a peek and saw it was empty. So that's what they were doing! I laughed out loud but felt a little sting of sadness that they didn't share this bit of information with me. It sure would have made my waiting time go by faster.

A few days later, I returned to our beloved pool. This time, I would make sure the older boys included me in their little game. I walked into the dressing room and noticed that the small wad was no longer there. In its place was a much larger wad. Had the hole gotten bigger, I wondered?

I went to my usual bench to sit and wait for everyone to finish changing. All the boys were naked, talking, laughing and happy to have another day of swimming and diving. The weather was once again perfect and nothing could possibly go wrong.

Nothing, that is, until the newspaper plopped on the floor. The hole was a few inches big and I could see something on the other side. Were those a pair of eyes? No, there were two pairs of eyes!

I yelped.

The naked boys looked at me when they heard my cry and all I could do was point towards the hole. Their heads turned ever-so-slowly and I watched as their jaws began to drop like flies. That's when panic set in. Boys began running from left to right as they frantically reached for anything that would cover their nakedness. Everyone was in a panic except me. I sat on my bench, comfortable and dressed, as a smirk slowly spread across my face. The girls had turned the table and had become the peepers. It was amusing, but it seemed that only the girls and I found it so.

My entertainment did not end that day. The fun volleyed back and forth between dressing rooms like an out of control bouncy ball. It didn't matter to me who was doing the peeping. I enjoyed the show fully dressed and from my favorite bench. This fun lasted until the manager found out about the constant fiasco in the rooms and quickly patched up the hole. It wasn't the first time and it wouldn't be the last time it was patched. Our gang (along with the girls) would continue to torment him with this matter.

That is until the manger finally got the upper hand.

A BUZZING AFFAIR

Caracas, Venezuela

The club manager finally had just about enough. It was time to finish it, and finish it he would.

According to him, there would be a minor change. Our old dressing rooms would be moved to a newer and larger facility. Not only would we have to walk a few more feet to get to the pool, but we would now have to share this new dressing room with adults (gulp). This would bring about some sort of supervision of both boys and girls. We had brought this on ourselves but that didn't make us any happier about the situation.

The new thirty-foot tall building was made out of cinder blocks, making everyone safe from holes in the wall mysteriously appearing. The only natural light entering the facility came from a few skylights nestled safely on the roof. Windows were conveniently left out of the design so to discourage any peeping. It appeared the manager had finally won the battle against our unruly bunch.

I thought that was the end of an era. Our boyhood was quickly turning into manhood as we were forced to behave like responsible adults.

But - there is always a but - not everyone was willing to give up so easily.

Our group was a good mix of age, which brought about varying levels of smarts and plain common sense. Some of us prided ourselves with common sense but there were a few who confused stupidity with genius. These brave boys, the same ones responsible for the fiasco in the bowling alley, had another awe-inspiring idea. Having examined the new building carefully, they came up with a scheme that would outlive the genius of their previous escapades. It would be a day every young boy on the verge of manhood would talk about for generations.

The plan went something like this: climb to the roof of the new dressing room building, slowly drill small peepholes into the women's dressing room skylights and sit back to enjoy the show. It sounded amazing to all the hormonally-charged boys around me, but I wasn't sold. It was too much for me and I decided to bow out and refrain from being involved in the trial run.

Climbing the roof was no easy task. The first obstacle was the fact that we weren't wearing anything other than a swimming trunk. It was training season for us and we would spend the entire day at the pool wearing our swim trunks, ready for practice at any time. Because getting a good grip without shoes was difficult, the group chose the best climber to go first. He began the dangerous and tiresome trek up the side of the building, all the while hauling a rope. Once on the roof, he hooked the rope to the wall and let it fall off the side. The rest of the boys had a much easier climb. The knots on the rope helped give them a strong grip and faster climbing speed.

Without me, the gang began their trip to the top of the building. They decided that in order to be less obvious, they would take turns, climbing on the roof in groups of three to four boys at a time. They were allowed a few minutes of viewing and would then have to switch with the next group. After witnessing a few successful trips, I gave in and decided maybe the idea wasn't too bad after all. I would make sure to join them during their next trip.

The following morning, my group was selected to go first. We approached the building, trying our hardest not to attract too much attention. We turned the corner and headed toward the back where our rope was usually located. We were stealthy, ducking into the bushes and walking in silence.

Upon reaching our destination, we noticed that our rope was no longer hanging from the building. We looked around frantically, hoping it had been moved but all we found was a nice ladder. We looked at each other and realized it was actually a blessing in disguise. The ladder was just the perfect height. We could easily climb to the top without any risk of falling to our death. We thought it was our lucky day. We were too young to realize that when something seems too easy, it probably isn't a good idea.

The first few boys climbed up. I was instructed to wait with the others. We decided it would be best if we moved back to the swimming pool until it was our turn. Why sit in a bush when we could be poolside? I soon took my place on the spring board, deciding to practice my dives.

None of us expected what would happen next. It was like something straight out of a horror story. At first, it sounded like a distant rumbling. I didn't pay much attention until I tuned in and realized the sound I was hearing was coming from humans.

The air was quickly filled with the sounds of boys screaming and wildly slapping at themselves over and over again. I quickly jumped down from the board and ran to see what was happening. As I turned the corner, I witnessed the club manager and two of his assistants carrying the ladder away from the building. I could hear the boys at the top shouting hysterically for them to return. The manager and his minions were undeterred and I could see a smirk plastered across his face that shouted "victory is mine."

The boys on the roof eventually found the rope. It had been pulled up and hidden out of sight. It took a few agonizing minutes for the first guy to inch his way down. He continued to scream during his entire descent, all the while crying out for his mom. The rest of the group followed, not doing any better than the first guy.

The boys slowly and painfully headed to the swimming pool and proceeded to walk in. The cool water seemed to soothe them. I ran up to them and asked what had happened. No words came from their lips. They didn't need to say anything. I could see the welts on their entire body and a few bees still clinging to their flesh. It was awful.

Apparently, the club manager got word of what we were up to. Upon hearing it, he decided enough was enough. All the yelling he had done through the years never seemed to get through to us so he decided it was time for action. We had declared war and war was not for sissies. He had ordered his men to strategically place some bee-filled honeycombs around the roof, pull up the rope and place the convenient ladder in its place. He knew what would happen next.

The lesson was learned. There would be no more attempts to repeat the same caper. We might not have had the best ideas, but we were smart enough not to repeat them. Besides, the manager took further precautions against our infiltrating the dressing room again. Not long after, barbed-wire was placed all around the perimeter of the roof, guaranteeing we would not return.

This was the first time in my competitive sport experience that I was glad I didn't come in first.

TOLLING BELLS

Calabozo, Venezuela

I pondered long and hard over whether or not I should disclose the location of the following story. Would anyone remember this tale from 1956? After weighing the risks involved in being recognized, I decided to go ahead and share where this took place. Calabozo is a small town located near an oil field out in the Venezuelan plains. It wasn't much to look at but it did provide some great hunting.

Super Dad and I arrived early in the morning before the sun even realized it was time to come up. We parked our car in a hidden location. We weren't so concerned with being seen, because hunting was allowed everywhere back then. Our concern was someone might like our car a little too much and take it for a spin.

Almost immediately upon exiting our vehicle, we knew we would be bombarded by a plethora of ticks and fleas, ready to pounce on any exposed part of our body, so we came prepared. Before departing, we had applied a generous amount of our own tick/flea-repelling substance: a full bottle of baby powder mixed with salicylic acid. The ointment was generously spread over our boots, pants, socks and any other piece of clothing we wore. It worked, but I would insist that you DO NOT try this at home! The mad scientist residing in both of us was almost always up to something, and it was usually something dangerous.

Our main goal that day was to hunt a jaguar. It was a big goal and one we didn't set lightly. Bringing one home would definitely improve our hunting reputation which needed a bit of boosting. Sometime into our trip, we came to accept we weren't going to get a jaguar. Instead, our booty consisted of rabbits, mosquitos, flies and a zillion other blood-sucking insects. We changed our strategy thinking it would help, but it only led to deer and snakes. Our third game plan worked like a charm. We chose to hunt peccary (wild pig) and lo and behold, we found success! We were able to capture one without incident. That said a lot for us! We had accomplished our goal.

Of course, everyone knows jungles are hot. Not only are they hot and humid, but they are difficult to traverse. Treading through dense jungle is incredibly laborious when attempting to do it with a large and heavy dead pig on your back.

How in the world do you carry such an animal out of the jungle? We didn't have a jungle-penetrating vehicle. It was just us, our weapons and our wits. I looked at Dad as he pondered our situation. My mind was blank and I relied on his wisdom to get us through. It didn't take long for his "eureka" moment to burst forth.

In excited and confident Italian, he stated "You get a strong branch. You tie the pig's front legs together and do the same with his hind ones. Then, you slide the branch between the legs and all the way through. One hunter picks up one end of the branch while the other grabs the opposite. See? Now, you walk."

His clever plan seemed to work, for a while at least. Unfortunately, something always went wrong with our hunting trips and this one was no exception. You see, wild pigs don't care about ticks or fleas; they do nothing to prevent them from climbing all over their bodies. Ticks and fleas are blessed with legs, meaning they don't sit contentedly in one place. No, that would be too easy and would make this story boring.

After hours of treading in the humid and wet jungle, our previously applied homemade tick/flea defense had worn thin. We had been so focused on hunting and carrying our prey, we had failed to pay attention to this minor detail. We were open to the elements and those elements were quickly moving off the peccary, onto the branch and down our arms and shoulders.

This was the day I learned the statement "flea bag" for two and four legged animals was a gross understatement. It did not even come close to describe the amount of tiny creatures inhabiting on our prey. Unfortunately, these creepy-crawlers do not discriminate between animals and humans, they gladly live on either.

Get the picture?

We did, too; and soon found ourselves with the dilemma of whether or not to forget the pig and run to the safety of our car. My dad was not one to give up easily so instead of abandoning it, we focused our energy on finding a way to get rid of the insects that were burrowing into our skin. The ticks were much more difficult to get rid of than fleas and if we wanted to do a thorough job, we would have to focus on each tick one by one. Our most accessible weapon was one of Dad's cigarettes. We lit one and brought it close to each tick until the heat caused it to let go and fall off which was advantageous as the entire tick was removed. Like everything in life, there was a down side to this method. The cigarette would eventually burn your skin, leaving a mark as a reminder of the encounter with nature.

Soon, we were tick-free and again on our way to our car, but enough time had passed that night was quickly approaching. It took twice as long to find all our landmarks in the dark. By the time we reached the car, it was much too late to drive home through the dangerous jungle and mountain roads, as roads back then did not contain as much light as they do now.

Instead, Dad, the pig, and I drove into town to rent a room for the night. We found one hotel in the main square of town. Our room was small with a single glassless window. Neither Dad nor I could see the bathroom but the hotel manager was quick to proudly inform us that they had a bathroom: it was called the outdoors.

We entered our room and scanned it with a careful eye. We were thankful that only a few of the outside elements could enter through the window, none of them large enough to cause us any serious harm. Before settling down for the night we made a trip to the "bathroom." On our way out, we stopped to ask the manager if they had a shower. He pointed his finger in the direction of a barrel full of water and walked back into the office. By this time, my dad and I were too tired to ask for more information. Instead, Dad stripped down to his underwear and dunked himself into the barrel. He bathed quickly and signaled me that it was my turn. I followed suit and climbed in, feeling refreshed almost instantly.

The peaceful moment was interrupted by shouting coming from the frantic manager as he ran towards us, bellowing at the top of his lungs. He was out of breath by the time he reached us and proceeded to explain that the barrel was not a bath, but merely a holding tank for the hotel's entire water supply. In our exhaustion, we failed to hear him the first time when he told us to use the small hollowed-out gourd (*totuma*) to douse ourselves with the water, outside of the barrel.

It was challenging to come to an agreement, but my dad resorted to his favored method of compromise. He simply paid the manager until the man was grinning from ear to ear, offering us a new barrel with clean water for our own personal use. "Let me know if you need more," he said as he walked back to his room with a skip in his step.

Finally, after one of the longest days of my life, we plopped our heads down on the pillows. Mosquitoes buzzed in and out of the glassless windows, happily stopping to say hi. We didn't care. We were glad to have a place to collapse and get our strength back. Sleep came quickly but didn't last.

At about five a.m., all the peace we were experiencing went flying out the window along with the plethora of mosquitoes when we were abruptly woken by the loudest tolling bells I have ever heard. Through the window, I could see the church bells ringing and ringing as if they would never cease. We couldn't fall back asleep with the incessant noise. No one in town seemed to care that we were drained. I could hear myself shouting, "Please stop!"

My dad heard me and he had a solution. He sat up, reached for his gun and shot a couple of slugs at the toiling bells, not missing a single shot. Every single one struck the holy bells and it was soon quiet once again. We lay back down, smiles spread across our faces.

It wasn't long before our new-found silence was broken by loud banging on our hotel room door. Dad reluctantly got up and dragged himself to open it. Somehow, we weren't really surprised to see the only police officer the town had. He had heard my dad didn't take well to the morning bells. He came to have a little talk with us and we soon found ourselves in the middle of another little "misunderstanding." The men spoke for some time and eventually, the officer left with a smile on his face. How did my dad do it? I'll leave it up to your imagination and deduction.

AIR, PLEASE!

Carenero, Venezuela

There are no words to describe the beauty of the coral reefs and mangroves at dawn. It is a breathtaking sight, and no matter how many times I was privileged enough to witness it, I was always in awe. On one particular day I remember well, the water was clear and green as emeralds. The coral, rocks and seaweed seemed to be at arm's reach, despite the fact they were about ten feet below the surface of the water. I could see the coral fish, sea urchins, snappers and stingrays in considerable numbers beneath our fifteen-foot aluminum boat. It looked perfect.

We had spent the night on the boat and woke up to what felt like a million itching mosquito bites. They were uncomfortable, but they wouldn't stop us from a day of snorkeling and spear fishing, especially since Dad was going to be testing his new toy. He had just purchased a new underwater full-body suit made out of neoprene. It looked like a big inner tube to me. It was heavy and only made worse by the full air tank that came with it.

I was excited to watch Super Dad wear his suit and spend a few hours pretending to be a submarine. I rigged a tarp to provide some shade, poured myself a cup of coffee, and stretched out my legs to get comfortable with a sandwich in hand that my mom had prepared for our excursion. This would be nice and relaxing, a perfect way to spend a hot day.

As I gleefully chewed, I noticed Dad looking at me. He had a surprised and quizzical look on his face. "What are you doing?" he asked.

My logical answer did not seem to suit him. "I am going to have a sandwich," I stated, "and wait for you to come back."

His reply was just as logical. "Are you nuts?"

I did not like the grin that spread across his face and asked him why he thought so.

"You should not eat before getting into that cold water," he said as his eyes conveyed another dangerous message.

"Dad, I am not planning on getting into the water. I'll just wait here until you return. I figured you purchased that suit for yourself and you alone would be wearing it."

He then hit me with his most logical statement of all: "Who, me? I am not going to try it on! You go first, and I may go after, if everything goes well with you."

Aha! There it was. I knew there was a catch behind all this logic. He wanted me to be the guinea pig. I did not like the idea one bit, but who was I to argue with him?

I got up and began the laborious task of donning the suit. It did not have any zippers and came in two separate parts. The top was like an extra-large t-shirt with a hood and the lower part looked like pants you would wear during a fresh water fishing expedition. It was just as awkward to put on as it was to look at.

I began with the top and soon found it would be a difficult task. Despite how large the shirt was, the designer decided that the hole for the head should only be large enough to allow an orange to pass through. I have always had an average-sized head so it surprised me when I couldn't get it on. No matter how hard Dad pushed, pulled and cursed, my head would not budge through the hole. It only took a few minutes of struggling before my dad had one of his genius ideas.

"We need some lubrication!" he exclaimed.

Before he finished his sentence, he began pouring a large amount of motor oil down my neck. This proved to be a brilliant move. My head easily and rather quickly swam into the shirt. I felt and looked like a sea lion, making me laugh out loud.

The laughter did not last long. The suit was snug and the rubber began to tighten around my neck. The smile on my face faded as I began to turn red. Dad told me to stop fooling around. I tried my hardest to tell him I was choking but the more I tried, the more amused he became. He didn't seem to notice that my face had gone from red to blue. He sat down to watch my performance and even began eating my sandwich.

My legs started to give out under me. Dad finally realized how much trouble I was in when I dropped down and almost tipped the boat over. He jumped up and frantically attempted to remove the shirt but failed at every attempt. My short life passed before my eyes. As my sight began to fade, I saw my dad grab his knife. Was he going mad? My bulging eyes were screaming "NO!"

Dad was quick. He cut around the neck so that I could breathe. My lungs expanded once again as I inhaled the warm tropical air. I sat catching my breath. I was a sight to see, with a neckless shirt and a severed hood on my head. Dad let me sit there until I felt better. It took a while for my natural color to return and for my dad to be able to relax. We sat in silence the whole time but once the situation seemed under control, he spoke.

"Are you ok?" Dad asked.

"Yes."

"Ok," he said slowly, "put on the rubber pants. You can dive now."

And so it was in my little world. You tried, you failed, you fixed what was broken and you tried again.

SHARK

Cabo Codera, Venezuela

I bought my first camera and began making home movies at the age of seventeen. Immediately I was hooked. I loved creating stories and watching them unfold from behind the camera. There were no digital cameras or editing software (heck, there weren't any computers). It was a tedious and time-consuming task to process pictures, and most people found it too difficult. I, however, was not like most people. Half the fun was the editing. I would film the title I had created, mostly from cardboard or magnetic letters on a magnetic board. I used my abilities as a cartoonist to add creative cartoon sequences where appropriate, and then would spend more time recording voices, sound effects and the like. I would then have to make sure the film was synchronized with the music/voices/sound effects. It was a lot of work but worth the time. So many years later, I still show those films to my grandchildren. They think I'm pretty cool and even make their own little films. It's a fun hobby I hope is handed down to their children.

In my late teens, I bought myself a new gadget: an 8mm set which included a camera and a projector. Despite my years of experience with filming, this set offered me a new challenge; it came with a special camera case for underwater filming. The case looked like a transparent American football. It was odd but I loved the idea that a whole new world of possibilities opened up for me.

This case had an opening on one of its ends, where I would have to place the camera inside and affix it with a few screws and butterflies. The camera would face the end of the case containing its own lens. The open end was sealed off with a glove-looking rubber piece, a gasket and another little gadget to seal it tight. The final step involved pumping air into the case using a bicycle pump. I was able to film, rewind and change lenses on the camera by turning a knob. Simple enough, right?

I was ready for my first underwater filming and I could hardly wait to try it out. Dad, on the other hand, was a bit more cautious. He would eventually tell me later that day that I should have known that it was not going to go as planned.

Regardless of my dad's "optimism," we headed out the door and soon found ourselves in our boat. We sped towards Cabo Codera for a nice, relaxing swim on the coast. However, it was the rainy season and living up to its wet reputation; the water was agitated and murky. In other words, most people with a shred of common sense would know that filming underwater in such conditions would be nearly impossible, as well as dangerous due to the fair share of predatory fish lurking below the surface.

My dad offered to lend me his diving suit for the underwater excursion. I graciously declined, ignoring the fact that my dad promised he had fixed it and it wouldn't try to kill me again. I had all I needed with my swimming mask and fins. I was pretty good at holding my breath thanks to all the swimming classes and meets under my belt. I put on all my gear and placed my hand in the rubber glove attached to the camera case.

Dad volunteered to be the star of my film. He was a strong, muscular man and would be perfect for our underwater theme. His spear in hand and his agile swimming moves rehearsed, he was ready to perform. Because we were responsible and modest, we made sure that his 1950s style tiny bathing suit was properly in place before diving in the water. We did not want any shocking surprises when the camera was rolling.

Dad jumped in, making a giant belly-splash. My entry was a bit gentler, since I was holding a camera and didn't want to break it on my first day.

I noticed there was a problem the moment I began my descent into the dark abyss. I would get as deep as half an inch and would float back up to the surface. I quickly realized that my attempts were being hindered by the fact that my fancy new camera case contained air. My body struggled to dive while my arm floated above the waves. This would prove to be difficult.

How in the world was I going to make my movie now? I could see Dad motioning me to follow him. His face showed frustration. His expression said "stop fooling around," but no matter how hard I pulled, I could not get my arm into the water.

My next move proved to be the most comedic of all. I placed my body on top of the camera, covering it with my stomach in an attempt to use my body weight to weigh it down. I was expecting this to work for at least a few inches of depth. It did not. I was so scrawny; anyone watching me would think I was rolling around on a ball floating on the surface of the ocean. The first few minutes of the movie were just shots of my unsynchronized water ballet.

My attempts were cut short when my dad spotted a shark. He signaled a warning and we headed to the safety of our boat. I had nothing of value filmed. My movie directing dream was over.

Night quickly came upon us. Dad eventually caught his shark but not while I was filming, of course. He hauled the five-foot shark onto our boat, making things rather messy and uncomfortable for the rest of the night. I was bitter for two reasons: I did not have a movie and I had to share my "bed" with a dead shark. It was certainly not what I had envisioned.

The next morning, Dad and I each had an idea. Mine was to go home and forget anything had happened. My dad, on the other hand, was thinking like a true filmmaker. He laid out his plan: pretend the dead shark was alive and film him fighting it. I jumped on the idea as fast as I had jumped in the boat the night before when we first spotted the shark. It would be my best and most realistic film yet!

My brother had joined us that morning and we put him to work on our little project. We placed the shark in the shallow water of the shore so that the dorsal fin would stick out. As I filmed, Dad swam up to it and rose out of the water with his knife in hand. The shimmer coming off the knife showed his intentions to terminate the beast. Dad began to stab the shark a number of times. He then wrestled and twisted the shark around in the water, giving the impression of a real man-vs-shark fight. At the end of the scene, he dragged the shark on shore, where he was a given a hero's welcome by my brother.

End scene.

I put the camera down and joined them to celebrate this momentous occasion. It was then I noticed the blood. This concerned me since the shark had been dead many hours and should not have been bleeding. I interrupted the celebration and pointed it out to my dad. He shrugged it off, stating that it was no big deal. Apparently, he had gotten a bit excited during the stabbing and had accidentally stabbed himself while fighting the dead shark. To him, it was just another battle wound. To me, it was my dad trying really hard to make his son happy.

After we were done celebrating and patching up Dad's self-inflicted stab wounds, we headed home eager to tell Mom all about our manly adventure. This would definitely go down in our family's greatest moments. I shuddered at the thought of what would have happened had the shark been alive. Of course, this was nothing to Super Dad. He wanted to be in my film and by golly, he was not only in it, but he had brought a great adversary with him.

Thank you, Dad!

SHARK, FOR REAL!

Carenero, Venezuela

It was safe to say, Dad had a real passion for fishing the wrong and dangerous way. It was also safe to say that I had the habit of following him with no complaints or questions. This, of course, led us to a new undertaking: spear-gun fishing.

Among the plethora of Dad's fishing gear were two spears that worked with black powder shells. The large and powerful one belonged to my dad while the smaller one was mine. The shells used in these spear guns were similar to those for shotguns, but smaller than and as thin as a pencil. They were inserted at the hollow end of the spear which was attached to a fifteen-foot bungee cord. The handle had a trigger that would set it into action. It was simple to use: place shells in chamber, aim, pull the trigger and away it went. It was a powerful shot that could easily wound a large fish at a distance of twenty feet.

Dad only waited one day before taking the spears out for a trial run. On the morning of our trip, he spent several long hours filling our shells with gun powder. He did his best to follow the instructions carefully. If not done properly, any little bit of moisture inside the shell would make them useless.

Our dynamic duo left the city and headed out for the small fishing town of Carenero. We arrived at our destination shortly before sundown. As was customary, we prepared to fish non-stop until morning. The cool evening air and the approaching darkness encouraged a variety of fish to come out of their hiding places. We wasted no time in baiting our hooks. The spears would wait until the early light of dawn.

My normal response to anything new Dad attempted was to feel nervous. Any time he had a new idea or purchased a new device, the butterflies in my stomach would begin to desperately climb up my throat and fly out of my mouth. New things usually equaled trouble.

By the time the first rays peaked over the horizon, Dad and I had already gone over our check list:

- ✓ Knife
- ✓ Mask
- ✓ Fins
- ✓ Spear guns
- ✓ Shells
- ✓ Bathing suits

It was time to go. In order to avoid capsizing, we simultaneously dropped into the water with the style and grace of a hippo attempting a yoga pose. It wasn't pretty but we got the job done. I was ready as soon as we hit the water. Dad immediately signaled me that he had something to say. I removed my mask and paid close attention.

"Do not bother with the small ones. These shells are expensive and we don't want to waste them on small catch."

He quickly put on his mask and was underwater before giving me the opportunity to make a suggestion. I thought it would have been a good idea to practice on a few small fish and get a feel for the spear guns. Oh, well.

It was obvious our task would be difficult from the first moment we dove down. The recent rains had left the water murky and our visibility was only about ten feet. I looked over at Dad as he nodded and gave me the ok to load a shell into the spear. How exciting!

We swam a few yards away from each other, looking around for our prey. What would it be? A large tuna? A fifty-pound bass? A minnow?

Time goes by fast when snorkeling. Despite the fact that our visibility was low, there was something relaxing about the entire experience. It felt like I was in a completely different world.

I glanced over to my dad just in time to see him give me the "V" signal. This meant there was a shark in close proximity. The water around me was suddenly warm (I'll let you use your imagination on that one). I turned my head slowly, once again seeing Dad signal. He pointed straight ahead of us. It was then I saw a large shadow in the murky water, swimming slowly as if trying to make my blood freeze with fear.

Much to my surprise, Dad pointed at the shark and signaled me to shoot. It was more like an order than a signal. Here was my dad, Tarzan-reincarnate, giving me the honor of the first kill. I did what was asked of me, aimed at the head and fired.

Nothing.

The shell failed to fire. In my panic, I looked over at Dad hoping to get some insightful information. All I got was another command to reload and shoot. I attempted a few more loads without success. I asked Dad to do the shooting and he proceeded to give the international sign for "go fly a kite." It was up to me and no one else.

The shark spotted us and quickly turned towards me. Panic came over me. I did the only thing I could think of under such dire circumstances. I closed my eyes and blew all the air in my lungs out into the snorkeling pipe. When I was done, I had a zillion bubbles in front of me. I did not want to see the open shark mouth coming towards me.

A few seconds passed. I felt a body pushing me and I could have sworn I was bleeding a river of blood.

This was surely the end! A few more seconds passed and there was still no pain.

Hmm....was I dead?

I opened my eyes and I saw Dad's smiling face giving me a strange look and pointing towards the boat. I swam faster than ever and quickly climbed into its safety. I scanned every inch of my body, checking to see if there were any injuries. I was okay! I asked my dad why he didn't shoot his spear while my life was in danger.

"I did before you did but it didn't work."

Laughter took over us. We most likely laughed due to nerves but it was good to release the tension that way. We came to the conclusion that either the shark wasn't hungry or he left because he got a side cramp from laughing at us idiots. We must have been a sight! Perhaps we found a break-through way to discourage hungry sharks: doing something stupid!

Of course, our day wasn't over. Dad refused to leave until we figured out what went wrong and were able to catch something using the spear guns. By this time, Dad's laughter had turned to anger directed at the guns. His mind could only focus on figuring out why they hadn't worked.

He took the long gun and loaded it with a new, dry shell. This time, he would test it outside the water. Apparently, dry shells work much better. He pointed up toward the sky and the instant he pulled the trigger, the stubborn spear shot out with a loud boom. It worked so well, in fact, that it broke the bungee attached to it.

We had no idea how far that thing could go until that very moment. We froze in shock and our mouths gaped in amazement. That was one powerful weapon! Eventually, the spear began coming down and landed upon the beach.

It impaled into the sand directly in front of a very muscular and mean-looking fisherman. This particular fisherman had a big, fast boat with him. The look on his face caused us to snap out of our trance. He furiously got into his boat and headed straight for us.

I have never seen, and surely never again saw, our little boat going that fast on such shallow water without the aid of an engine. It's amazing the strength humans can muster up when they fear their lives are in danger.

P.S. If you are wondering, those spear guns were never used again.

JAGUAR 1, HUNTER 0

Caracas, Venezuela

I'm sure by now it is obvious how much I enjoyed time with my dad. No matter where we went or what kind of risky adventure he took me on, I was always willing to be at his side. Endless hours were spent in bushes, boats and trees hunting for jaguars, peccary and tapir, but never getting anything but rabbits and ducks. Despite how much we loved these escapades, there were times when we needed to spend our "quality" time in the zoo, where it was often safer for the animals and for us.

By 1957, my parents had reproduced one again, this time giving me a little sister. I enjoyed having her around much more than I would have when I was younger. She had no idea what she got into when she joined our family. With time, she would come to realize her mistake, but during one particular outing, she was pretty oblivious to what took place.

El Paraiso Zoo was not what you would think of a zoo today. Even in its day, it was still different compared to other zoos but it was well populated with a variety of animals. There were animals from various parts of the world, but the majority of them were native to Venezuela, including: snakes, caimans, capybara, tapirs, peccaries, monkeys, birds, pumas, black panthers and our favorite, the jaguar.

The animal cages were not very pretty to look at. In fact, most animal activists of today would have a heart attack if they were to travel back in time and if they recovered, they would then tie themselves to the cage in protest. The containment units were small, dirty and stunk worse than the poop thrown by the devious monkeys.

If hungry, the zoo provided its attendees with a "restaurant" as some called it. It was a small eatery with a variety of local and Italian food. The menu included a good supply of sodas and beer. It was a popular eatery, often visited by zoo patrons and almost always frequented by roaches.

After arriving, we ate lunch and began to make our round through the zoo. Our first stop was the monkeys. What kid doesn't want to see the monkeys first? We proceeded to not only observe, but to do our usual mimic of them. We acted like idiots to get them to perform, and threw candy at them as a reward (an allowed practice back then). They never failed to entertain.

When we tired of the monkeys, we moved on to our favorite exhibit, the jaguar cage! If our family were to have a family crest, there would most likely be a jaguar on it. We loved how powerful and beautiful the animal was. Dad especially loved the challenge it provided every time he would hunt for one. It was a love/hate relationship he had. He loved the idea of catching one, but hated the fact that he never did.

We all arrived at the cage and proceeded to talk in excitement at being able to be so close to the creature. The large female jaguar was lying down with her back against the bars. This was the closest we had ever been to a jaguar we weren't running away from or trying to shoot. She was at arm's length, which caused my brother much pleasure.

He decided it would be great fun to tease and torment this large, spotted cat. He was most likely thinking that teasing the monkeys was safe enough so why not the jaguar? After all, she was in a cage, so what harm could she do? He began his plan by throwing a little paper ball at her. She remained unmoved so he moved on to step two. He grabbed his soda, shook it a bit and sprayed her with it. Dad wisely asked him to stop. My brother, unwisely, proceeded.

This bombardment dragged for a while. She continued to keep her back turned at my intelligent brother and refused to react to any effort he made.

A few minutes passed, and the jaguar decided it was time to move, as she was tired of my brother's tormenting and knew she had the greatest weapon of all. She calmly stood up and slowly turned away from my stupidly smiling brother. The spotted cat then began to wiggle her tail just enough to send a powerful spray of stinking urine that showered my brilliant sibling from head-to-toe, including his smiling face.

There he stood, soaking wet with rancid jaguar pee. The stench was unbearable and made it difficult for any of us to hold down the lunch we had just eaten. None of us wanted to be near him and anyone who walked by would quickly realize their mistake. We voted on whether or not we should allow him in the car with us for the ten mile ride home; but in the end, my mom's love won and he got to come home with us. We drove with our windows rolled down and our heads sticking out.

Most people think that skunk smell is the worst but they have obviously never smelled jaguar urine. It took a long time for my brother's normal smell to be restored. It took just as long for me to be able to sleep soundly because we shared a room. My mom washed bedsheets every day and nagged my brother about scrubbing hard when he went to shower. Soon enough, the smell faded into a distant memory, but my brother's legacy lives on to this day.

These are the kind of memories I am glad I still have.

FISH HUNTERS

Carenero, Venezuela

Carenero was a fisherman's paradise and full of character. It was a small town, and besides the usual buildings found in coastal population, Carenero had an old abandoned train station that gave the place a unique look. No one knew exactly when the trains stopped running, but seeing nature reclaim the station and tracks showed earth's powerful force in the battle against civilization.

The coastline in these parts contained small and large lagoons surrounded by mangroves. The waters were filled with catfish, tarpons, snuck, bass, snappers, moray eels, cutlass fish, sardines and mullets. There was a likely chance we could catch our dinner when fishing in Carenero. On the occasion we didn't catch

171

anything, the beautiful scenery would make up for any disappointment. It was truly a tropical paradise.

To enjoy a day of fishing, we took out Dad's aluminum fifteen-foot boat. By this time, he had equipped it with a small sixteen-horsepower outboard motor and two oars. Night fishing was our thing, and in order to accommodate our all-nighters Dad had rigged it with some pine boards strategically placed across the boat seats to serve as beds. These boards weren't wide. When we laid on them, our shoulders would dangle off the sides. It wasn't comfortable but one could rest a bit during the long night hours (which would often turn into days).

The tropical nights were cool and on most nights, you could see every single star, planet and comet above. Below us, the phosphorous streaks left by large fish could be seen. On the occasional moonless night, the millions of phosphorescent dots filling the water gave the appearance that the sky and the water melted into each other. It was breathtaking. Other nights, lighting would surround our small boat. Dad always sat back and enjoyed the show while I worried whether we would make it through the night.

Despite how beautiful it was to sit in the dark, we would still require some sort of light. Putting the bait on the hook could be tricky and could lead to an accidental finger hooking if done blindly. Light was also needed in order to safely unhook the fish, not so much for the fish's sake, but for our sake when we were dealing with moray eels, barracudas and sharks. Light meant safety, at least most of the time. There was the occasion when fish would find it amusing to dart out of the water towards the light, hitting us like arrows. It was funny, but only when you managed to get away without being pierced by one of those little beasts. They were a type of needle-nosed fish that are strangely attracted to bright lights, and if you happen to be in their path, too bad for you.

Anyway, this story is not about the fish. It's about what happened the next morning.

We spent the first three to four hours of sunlight snorkeling through the clear water. We would often spear our prey during this time of the day, all the while enjoying the sights the underwater world provided. We took our "lunch" break soon after. I say "lunch" because I don't want to get into descriptions of anything that might upset those with sensitive stomachs. So, we will leave it at "lunch."

After chowing down our meal, we decided to continue our fishing from the boat. We rowed into one of the larger lagoons, knowing that the fish there probably hadn't learned of our presence. We were trolling along when Dad caught a gigantic tarpon. Before I go any further, it would be beneficial to remember that when we fished from the boat, we did not use fishing rods. We would hold the fishing line with our bare hands, often leading to burns and cuts due to the constant pulling of the nylon line.

Tarpons can be as long as eight feet and weight as much as two hundred and eighty pounds and ours was no wimp. He was about five feet long. He was giving Dad quite a fight, causing much injury to his hands. He looked around for a solution and quickly found one in me.

"Here!" he shouted. "You hold the line."

I couldn't argue an order given directly by Super Dad, Master and Commander. The tarpon was as big as I was, and I could only imagine it must have been on steroids. I reluctantly grabbed the line and immediately began my struggle with the giant beast. The moment I took over, dad grabbed his shotgun. The tarpon continued his fight and dad took aim at the water.

Have you ever had a moment in your life that plays itself in slow motion because it seemed so surreal? This was one of those moments. In slow motion, the tarpon leapt out of the water high above our heads. His scales glimmered in the sunlight. His five-foot body shook from side to side and appeared to be suspended in mid-air. Dad aimed, shot a few rounds into the giant and down it came. The fishing line now had plenty of slack. No more pulling and struggling.

There was no room for him in the trunk due to his enormous size. Dad did the next best thing and tied him to the hood of the car. We drove home with our prize catch for the entire world to see. This one did not get away. He was our dinner guest for an entire week's worth of dinners despite his poor flavor. I got no credit for my bleeding hands or for being the one to gut that monstrosity.

Dad, on the other hand, had a story. For many years, he told anyone who would listen about the day he "hunted" a fish.

JAGUAR 2, HUNTER 0

El Sombrero, Venezuela

Although it seems like yesterday, this one particularly memorable hunt happened in the late 1950s. Super Dad and I were hunting on a pitch dark, moonless night. We were on our usual mission: to catch anything that moved. This usually meant we would head home with a few rabbits if we were lucky. We were prepared for anything with our usual arsenal of weapons, which included one twelve-gauge shotgun, one sixteen-gauge, and two hunting knives. To complete whatever hunting gear we lacked, we invited my dad's friend to come along. His nickname was "El Polaco" which in Spanish means "The Polish One." El Polaco added to our supply list with his WWI model VW Jeep, huge cooler, one twenty-two rifle, a BB gun and a few shotguns.

Unfortunately, my little brother was the last one to complete our group. I say this because to my embarrassment, he witnessed the following story and happily repeated it as many times and to as many people as he could. This was probably revenge for the time I told everyone about his adventure with a jaguar. Karma sucks.

We began our journey threading through a maze of dirt roads. We wore our search lights (more like modest head lamps but a boy can dream, right?), looking for any pair of eyes that would glitter in reflection to our light. We were getting pretty good at distinguishing which color of eyes belonged to which animal. We had learned the hard way (a story I don't wish to comment on) that blue eyes usually indicated a cow or wild donkey. Deer also had blue eyes, but we had not seen their likes in the area for quite some time. It was safe to say, we did not shoot at blue eyes.

El Polaco was our driver and I was fortunate enough to be seated in the passenger seat. This had proven to be the best shooting position and I held on to it proudly despite the fact I had not actually earned it. Super Dad and my brother sat in the back seat as we inched our way through the jungles. We drove in what felt like endless circles. Rabbits were the only animals falling victim to our hunt so I decided to get some sleep. Most of our trips were like these, so you can imagine my surprise when Dad woke me up.

"Jaguar at two-o'clock!" he whispered in an excited voice.

That was on my side of the Jeep! I quickly became alert and listened to his further instructions.

"Go for it! She is resting over there, just about thirty feet from here."

I grabbed a gun without looking. I jumped out of the Jeep and in my excitement (a.k.a. fear), I failed to pay attention to where I was stepping. I could have waked into a pile of snakes and not realized it. I was focused and the only thing on my mind was the jaguar. I moved closer to the red eyes. It was a big one, the mother of all jaguars! I was so close that even with my feeble head light, I could see the spots on her skin. I slowly raised my weapon to aim. I knew it would be an easy shot, right between the eyes. The moment I took aim, reality hit me. In my excitement and half-asleep state, I had not grabbed a shot gun or a rifle as any sane person would have done. No. Not me. I grabbed the BB gun.

According to the three witnesses, this is what happened next.

The moment I realized I had put myself in danger by grabbing a harmless weapon, I began to do what I deemed best. I began to go back to the Jeep in the same manner I walked out. I didn't turn my back on the jaguar. With my arms raised and useless weapon still pointed at her, I walked backwards without a glance, only aiming and staring at the beast in front of me. I eventually and miraculously reached the

Jeep without tripping or stepping on any other creature. I sat, put the gun in its original position, and stared forward without a word or a blink of an eye. The jaguar waited for me to settle, as if she knew that no harm would come to her. She got up and walked away, probably annoyed at the loud laughter coming from our hunting party.

We continued through the jungle for another hour. My companions' laughter didn't show signs of stopping as I suffered from cold sweats at the thought of what could have happened. Much to my despair, the night was not over. We continued driving at our snail's pace in hopes of catching something other than rabbit.

Suddenly, El Polaco stopped the Jeep. Dad handed me the rifle.

"There you have a rabbit, just straight ahead. Get it. It won't bite you!" he said in a serious tone, but I could clearly see, even in the dark, the laughter behind that stern face.

I would not fail him this time. I couldn't fail. I stepped out of the jeep and raised my weapon. I pulled the trigger and watched the bullet cross less than an inch away from the rabbit's nose. It leapt towards me and I shot again. I missed. The rabbit kept hopping towards me. Once it was about fifteen feet away, I shot and yes, I missed again. The rabbit continued its approach and reached my feet. It was a guaranteed shot. I almost shot my own foot and much to my amazement, I missed. Again.

Everyone we knew came to hear this embarrassing tale. My brother reveled at having a jaguar story of his own to embarrass me with. It has been more than fifty-seven years since that fateful night, and I can still hear those never-ending belly laughs. They travel through time, reminding me to always look before I leap.

CABO CODERA

Cabo Codera, Venezuela

Smack in the middle of the Antilles Sea coast of Venezuela, Cabo Codera protrudes out to the sea. Its position makes it a challenging place for small boats to cross due to the currents coming from all sorts of directions. It is difficult enough in good weather, so you can imagine how much more difficult this would be in bad weather. The water there is cold and relatively deep. A large number of boats, both large and small, have seen their last on those rocky shores. Most boats passing by stay clear of the cape by at least a mile and pray that their engine doesn't malfunction.

Back in the 60s, there were no beacons or signal buoys. There were no cell phones, GPS or the like. Surviving a crash or hoping for rescue would depend on personal skills and whether or not there were any witnesses to call for help. Despite the fact that this place was frequented by *coletazos* (the tail end of a hurricane passing by) there were no systems in place for warning sailors of any oncoming major storms. As you can tell, this was not for the faint of heart.

Despite all that, there was also a deep beauty in that place: the cape itself was breathtaking and the variety of creatures and beautiful flora was matched by few locations. The rocks looked white in the sunlight, mostly because of the blanching done by pelican and seagull guano. There was a constant presence of mantas and devil rays playing in the water and sharks feeding on large fish. It was proof of the never-ending survival game of the sea.

The nights offered a beautiful display of the cosmos. This beauty melded into the sea with the glowing, phosphorescent creatures. It was important to keep in mind the dangers of the place because one could easily get lost in its beauty.

By this time, I was twenty-four and married to my college sweetheart. Margarita and I had dated for four-and-a-half LONG years and married just three months after graduation. It was a monumental achievement not only because she actually said yes, but because we had both received our doctorate in Pharmacy. It was a blissful time in my life and what better way to celebrate than to experience another outing with Dad.

This time, he chose a far-from-perfect night to go fishing. Why, you ask? Because Super Dad loved the challenge such an adventure would bring. Being older and wiser, I should have known better than to say yes, especially when my pregnant wife decided she wanted to join us. My father was delighted to have her. I, on the other hand, began a long night of worry.

Long ago, Dad had upgraded our aluminum boat that held so many fond memories for a larger one containing a cabin below. The cabin was large enough for two cots and nothing else. It made night fishing much more comfortable. We loaded up our boat with the usual supplies, this time bringing blankets for the cold night. Upon our arrival, I noticed the sky and was positive that a storm was coming from the east. Margarita didn't care. Dad was happy. I was concerned because even though the water in the bay was calm, I could see that further out the waves were coming from two different directions, which usually led to my severe sea-sickness.

We got the boat in the water and the engine started like a dream. We usually had to fight to get it going, which made me hopeful and thought that maybe this excursion wouldn't be so bad.

It only took Dad an hour to find the perfect fishing spot. It was starting to get dark by the time I dropped the anchor at a depth of approximately twenty feet. With every minute that went by, the water seemed to get choppier. My stomach soon began to shout for mercy and I had no idea how long I would be able to hold on to its contents.

Dad and I soon began to work with our lines and sinkers, placing our bait on the hook. Since we didn't use fishing poles, we had finally discovered that using a small rag would protect our hands in case a fish happened to put up a fight. It's probably considered primitive in today's fishing standards, but it got the job done and kept our bellies filled.

While we worked on the fishing equipment, Margarita began to make us sandwiches. Not wanting to be left out, Dad pitched in with the meal preparations and pulled out the wine bottle. No meal would be complete without a ration of homemade soup so my wife served us each a cup. To celebrate our filling meal, Dad poured more wine. After all, it was the proper Italian thing to do.

We ate, we drank, we laughed and then all hell broke loose. My wife noticed the color on my face quickly began to fade into a pasty-green befitting a corpse. It was promptly followed by a dizzy spell, cold chills and… well, you get the picture.

I decided to head down below and lay down on the cot so my stomach could settle. I'm sure this idea would have worked if it had not been for what took place in the cabin earlier that day. You see, Dad had lent his boat to some friends the previous week. They had taken a fishing expedition of their own, but had failed to clean the boat out. Left alone for the week in the tropical heat, the combination of garbage and fish guts made a nice recipe for cockroach food. When Dad went to prepare the boat for our trip, he decided that the best thing to do, besides clean it out, was to bomb the boat with bug spray. The trick worked and all roaches either jumped ship or died. The mess was gone but no amount of cleaning could remove the putrid smell of rotten garbage enveloped in toxic bug spray.

I noticed the smell too late. I had already laid my weak body down and found myself too sick to go out to the fresh air. Margarita had been smart and remained above. No matter how much she beckoned me to come up, I couldn't move. It was awful and there was nothing I could do about it.

Meanwhile, my seven-month pregnant wife was having the best fishing trip of her life. She was so successful that my dad's sole job was to keep baiting her hook. He had no time between her catches to get his hook prepped. In less than two hours, she managed to fill our eighty-pound cold chest with a plethora of fish. This was an amazing feat of strength for someone who had never before caught anything weightier than a few ounces. Needless to say, Dad was having a ball: his daughter-in-law was fishing like a champ while his son was spewing like Mount Vesuvius. For many years after, he would tell people "my son lost as many pounds as my daughter caught in fish."

Funny, Dad. Funny indeed.

Eventually, the storm passed as we settled into the night. The cold chest was filled to the brim with fish as Dad sat contently with a glass of wine in one hand and a cup of coffee in the other. My wife had a smile that spread across her face with the satisfaction of the night's accomplishments. Everyone was happy expect sick little me.

Early morning came and even before the sun was up, Dad gave me the order to reel in the anchor. I was still feeling the effects of the storm, but managed to get up and begin the laborious task. I pulled, it stayed put. No matter how hard I tried, it would not budge. Dad's patience began to wear thin. In order to avoid offending my wife, he called me a name in the Italian dialect we spoke. I believe the word was *stronzo*. He made his way over and began to try to pull it up himself.

"It's stuck!" he cried.

"I know," I sighed.

He turned the motor on and maneuvered the boat from side to side in an attempt to loosen the anchor from its resting place. It seemed clear that it was not even moving an inch. I suggested the next best thing, cutting the cord.

"Are you nuts?" Dad said as he looked at me with one of those looks that could kill a person on the spot. Fortunately for me, I was used to these looks and was rather immune to them.

"That anchor is almost new!" In my dad's vocabulary, "almost new" meant that he had recently found it and despite the fact it was rusted over, it was still a step up from the concrete-filled can we had been using.

It was still dark so Dad asked me to use a flashlight.

"Dad, how could a flashlight help?"

A loud splash was soon followed by the statement "*stronzo doppio.*" *Doppio* means double. Whatever name he had called me before, my wife knew I had been called it again times two.

After Dad jumped into the dark and treacherous water, he proceeded to ask me to point the light towards the anchor. I knew the anchor was too deep to be illuminated by my feeble flashlight but I saw no point in arguing with him. I did what was asked of me and Dad quickly submerged. He began following the ray of light into the abyss. I looked at my wife and could easily tell she was concerned by the roundness of her big brown eyes.

A minute went by.

Two minutes went by.

I knew Dad could hold his breath three minutes because I had been working hard to beat his time. It was an impressive record, but one I knew would be difficult to match in the deep, cold water. As Margarita's concern turned into panic, I began to ready myself to jump in after him.

189

Suddenly, we heard loud splash behind us. We ran to other side of the boat and immediately felt relieved upon seeing Dad's face.

"Ok," he stated breathlessly, "the anchor is free, so go pull the rope."

I began to work with ease. The rope seemed to be effortlessly coming up. I thought maybe I had misjudged the depth seeing how much slack was on the rope.

"Hurry!" Dad shouted.

I was confused. I wasn't sure why my dad was in such a rush seeing that we had the rest of the day to get home so I asked him why.

"Because I'm holding the anchor in my arms!"

I know that objects are lighter in water but this was a thirty-plus pound anchor and he had just swum into the deep water for three minutes while holding his breath. Dad had freed the anchor and in order to avoid further problems, he figured the next logical thing to do was for him to bring it up. I told you he was part superhero.

If I did not have my wife as a witness, I would most likely question my memory of Dad's powerful feat of strength. Fortunately, I have never forgotten the lessons I learned that night/day:

1. Dad was strong.
2. Dad was fearless.
3. My wife knows how to fish.
4. The fish she caught were delicious.
5. One must be nuts to go fishing with Dad.

Oh, and by the way, we lost the anchor during our next fishing expedition.

THE HORSE

Guadeloupe, French Islands

I have always loved horses. If an opportunity was presented to me where there would be a horse involved, I would be the first one to raise my hand shouting "Me! Me! Me!" at the top of my lungs. I loved them as a child, as a teenager, as an adult and even when circumstances were far from perfect.

I had been married two years when my sweetheart and I decided to go on our first overseas vacation, leaving our young son with her parents. The excitement of our coming trip was nothing compared to the nerves I felt at the thought of flying for the first time. Margarita was a seasoned flier, having traveled by plane several times inside Venezuela and twice to Spain. I, on the other hand, was not thrilled at placing my life in the hands of the pilot and a metal bird that couldn't even flap its wings.

Despite my reservations, we boarded a brand-new Boeing 707. I managed to hold it together enough not to run up and down the isles with excitement when the plane finally reached our destination, the French island of Guadeloupe. Of course, as in previous stories, I will leave out the name of the resort and those involved to avoid embarrassment.

This island was, and I'm sure still is, a paradise. The long beaches with its fine white sand stretch out for miles. One could easily idle away the days enjoying the leisurely pleasures of lying under the palm trees and wading in the blue-green warm waters. They were constant reminders that we were in the Caribbean. The warm breeze seemed to blow these days by quickly.

Despite the leisurely feel to the island, we decided to stick to a strict schedule in order to get the most of our vacation. Our time was limited and we wanted to make sure we did all we set out to do. These activities included:

- Swimming
- Post-swimming napping
- Fishing
- Post-fishing napping
- Sipping fresh coconut milk with rum
- Post-drinking napping

- Dancing to Caribbean music
- Post-dancing napping
- Water skiing
- Eating as much as possible (especially the lobsters we caught and cooked right on the beach with the help of a local chef)
- Horseback riding on the beach
- Post-napping napping

Needless to say, we were living life to the fullest.

One fateful day, I learned that a guest at the resort was ill with a horrible sore throat, fever and chills. The only local doctor flew from island to island in a small, two-engine plane whenever he was needed. Unfortunately for the ill patron, he was currently away and would not be bothered to return just for a sore throat. It was then that the pharmacist in me came out. I volunteered my services and quickly prescribed the much needed antibiotics. We went to the only pharmacy in town and were soon informed by the clerk that the pharmacist was out fishing. No problem, I thought. I confidently walked behind the counter, searched through the shelves and easily found the required antibiotic. I had fulfilled my duty as I had promised to do when I took my oath as a pharmacist.

The next day, I was proclaimed "Resort Hero."

A few days went by. We continued to fully dedicate ourselves to our schedule and hoped to enjoy the remainder of our vacation without further interruption. This hope was short lived. We were soon approached by the hotel manager. I could see she had been crying as she tried to hold back further tears. Something deep down inside told me not to get involved, but due to my hero status, I had no choice. She did not speak any language I knew and in turn, she could barely understand mine. In hindsight, I see now that I understood a lot less than I thought.

The island had only a few horses, six at most, and hers had been hit by a car the previous night. My services were requested. It is here I must once again disclose my profession. I studied pharmacy and microbiology, not veterinary medicine. I just wanted to make that clear to my readers before I continue with this most unfortunate of tales.

I soon found myself following the distraught manager. A few steps into our journey, I noticed that more and more guests began to join us at the rear of the procession. The closer we got to the injured horse, the more uncomfortable I became. Nothing good could come of this, I thought to myself. What did I get myself into? Whatever was going to happen would unfold front of all those people. Gulp.

We reached the victim. He was lying on his side, head flat on the ground and breathing heavily. I immediately noticed a large laceration on his belly, most likely in the general area where the guts would be. A crude attempt at stitching the cut had been made, using the horse's own hide. I could see that his eyes were alert and aware of his surroundings. I can only image the pain he must have been in.

After struggling some more with the language barrier, I gathered more information on the situation. The veterinarian, probably the same island doctor, had flown in to fix the horse but had just as quickly left for another island. From what I understood, he had given the horse a few shots, most likely an anesthetic.

I looked at the manager and at the growing circle of people around us as I took in a breath big enough to allow me to give my verdict. The air was filled with silence as every ear around me strained to hear what I had to say.

"The horse's weight is pressing on his lungs," I proclaimed in my wisest voice. "This is the cause for his breathing difficulty. On the other hand, the horse is afraid of moving, let alone standing, due to the anesthetic injection so close to his legs. I believe he should be standing up by now."

This horse was big. It was an English pure-bred horse and in order for me to help it up, I would need a few good Samaritans to assist. At first, only one came to my rescue but after watching us pull, push, and sweat with no results, a few more stepped up to the plate.

Approximately three hours later, dusk began descending upon the island. The beauty of it must have inspired our friend the horse, because it was at that moment when he finally managed to stand up. All our efforts had paid off. I could hear quiet whispers surround me. "It's a miracle!" they said. The excitement among the crowd built, and as they prepared to deliver a round of applause, the horse looked me straight in the eye and dropped dead.

Silence.

The crowd slowly dispersed, giving me dirty looks as they walked away. Their glaring eyes quietly asked, "How could you do it?" I could feel the manager's eyes drill a huge hole in the back of my skull. I did not dare turn. Pretty soon, I found myself alone and staring at my dead patient. I dared to look around for Margarita. Surely, I could depend on her support. Unfortunately, she had been one of the first people to leave the crime scene. I had no other choice but to wait for full darkness to come to my aid. Once it was upon me, I felt brave enough to dart to my room, skipping dinner. I snuck in, finding my wife conveniently asleep.

I awoke painfully early but stayed in bed for a very long time. I was afraid to face the world and what it would hold for a horse-killer such as me. Despite my best efforts to hide, hunger got the better of me, and I decided I needed nourishment.

On my way to the cafeteria, I bravely managed to look into the faces of a few of the guests. Surprisingly, I noticed that they no longer held gazes of anger, but gentle and friendly smiles. I nearly fell over with shock when I saw the manager. Instead the hate-filled glare I expected, I was greeted with a friendly "good afternoon." Was last night a nightmare? I had spent the entire morning thinking of the huge bill I would be receiving for the cost of a new fine-bred horse. Why was everyone being so nice?

Eventually, I was approached by a guest who took the time to explain the events that took place during the wee hours of the morning, causing the change in everyone's mood. The doctor had returned to the island and explained to the manager and other witnesses that he had not expected the horse to survive. He had experienced bad internal bleeding and was expected to suffer a great deal before dying. As a matter of fact, the doctor had returned to the island to put the horse to sleep so he wouldn't suffer any more.

This led to the renewed sense of my heroism. I had given the horse a good death. He left the world proudly, on all fours, as all noble horses should. I had inadvertently given him back his dignity. I allowed him to die quickly and without further suffering. A true hero, indeed!

I slept like a baby that night.

The rest of our vacation went on without a hitch. We enjoyed our remaining time in paradise and the perks that the rank of hero brought. Everyone spoke of my brilliance and good deeds. I was more realistic and quietly kept a secret to myself: I wasn't special, I just got lucky.

CONCLUSION

One day, I discovered the sky.

I mean, I had seen the sky before: it was blue. But this time, it was different. My childhood had ingrained in me the fact that bombs fell from the clouds. It was on that day I realized the connection in my mind between the bomb-filled airplanes and the sky above. Before then, those powerful explosions which made the ground tremble, and buildings burn and turn to rubble, were just explosions.

The revelation I had did not come instantly. It was a series of linked events leading me to see the sky in a different way. Throughout my life, whenever I saw people running, I looked up at the sky above. Whenever I heard the sounds of explosions, I looked up regardless of their real source. My knowledge of the everyday sky was filled with dog fights, search lights, explosions, tracer bullets, falling planes and round white parachutes.

At the end of the war, when Berlin was falling, the radio was broadcasting terrible news: children were among the last remaining defenders of the great city. I looked at the sky, clear blue with small sheep-like clouds. To this day, every time these little clouds float by, I remember that day.

Much later in life, after my wife and 4 children had moved to Miami, Hurricane Andrew paid us an unpleasant visit. It was in the late hours of the evening when the sky was pitch black that I began to chop down a small tree broken by the increasing winds. I looked up at that sky and saw ever-darkening clouds coming at an incredible speed towards our home. It was a fantastic yet frightful whirlpool of darkness. A few hours later, I rushed indoors as the full and brutal force of the hurricane hit our home without mercy. Needless to say, every time I see a dark cloud wandering in the sky, my mind goes back to that fateful day.

Life continued to provide more occasions to remember the sky: some bad and some good.

Fishing and hunting with my dad gave me plenty of opportunities to look upon the night sky. I would spend these stargazing nights in a small fishing boat with Dad. Often after the conversations died and our fishing continued in silence, I could see the unlimited tropical sky and would often look to Sirius, my favorite star. As I gazed upon this spectacular star, my mind would freely wander, looking for clues on how my future would unfold.

Those long childhood meditations were consistent: I wanted to have a family, a wife to share the rest of my existence. I did not speculate on my wife-to-be's features. We would have a small house with a small yard. A car was a must but not too big. Children? Yes. A horse? Maybe.

These dreams continued for years with the passing of time and age adding a few more details. It was a project in the making. While attending university, a new student joined our class. She was a month late because she had been studying in Madrid, Spain. She had transferred to Venezuela, her home. It was then, when I first saw her, that I saw Sirius in her eyes.

More than fifty-seven years later, I still see Sirius in the same places: in the sky and in her eyes.

Dear Reader,

I wanted these stories to come to life and thought that pictures would help do that. It was difficult to select which ones to include because there are so many I wanted to share. After much sorting and consulting with my dad, here are the final choices. Enjoy!

Carolina S. Barr

Brian K. Barr created the book cover using this picture as a starting point. It was taken by my uncle during the infamous Shark movie story. I love how my dad is posing as my grandpa focuses on the journey ahead.
Carenero
Circa late 1950s

This is one of my favorite pictures. It shows my dad holding my great-grandpa's hand as they cross Via Udine. I often tease Dad about having worn lederhosen-looking pants.
Trieste, Italy.
Circa 1942

This is a great picture of my dad, looking rather dapper, during one of his many expeditions into the Venezuelan jungle.
Silla de Caracas.
Circa late 1950s

There is no such thing as a cool day in the hot
and humid jungle.
Silla de Caracas
Circa late 1950s

Here is Dad showing off with one of his epic dives. This picture was taken at the same pool he often frequented as a youth. It makes me wonder if the pool manager was keeping an eye on him while he dove for this picture.
Casablanca Club
Circa late 1950s

The horse in this picture was a Columbian Paso Fino horse that lived in the area of Santa Lucia. Fortunately for this horse, it never needed my dad's medical assistance for anything. That's probably why it lived so long.
Santa Lucia
Circa early 1970s

A family friend who frequented the Guarenas Country Club had two pet jaguars, one male and one female. They often traveled with them when staying at the club for the weekend. This picture shows dad holding the male jaguar. He had originally wanted to pose with both the jaguars but his friends told him he would be crazy to do so. I guess since he only posed with one, you could say he's only half crazy.
Guarenas Country Club
Circa mid 1950s

32960284R00120

Made in the USA
San Bernardino, CA
20 April 2016